BIZARRO HEROES

BOOM
BOOM

by Dan Piraro

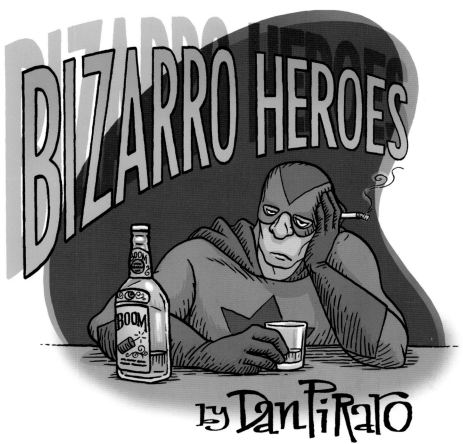

Bizarro is syndicated internationally by King Features Syndicate, Inc. For information, write King Features Syndicate, Inc., 300 West Fifty-Seventh Street, New York, NY 10019.

ISBN: 978-0-86719-756-3

Printed in China

Last Gasp
777 Florida Street
San Francisco, CA 94110
www.lastgasp.com

This book is lovingly dedicated to my own insecurities.

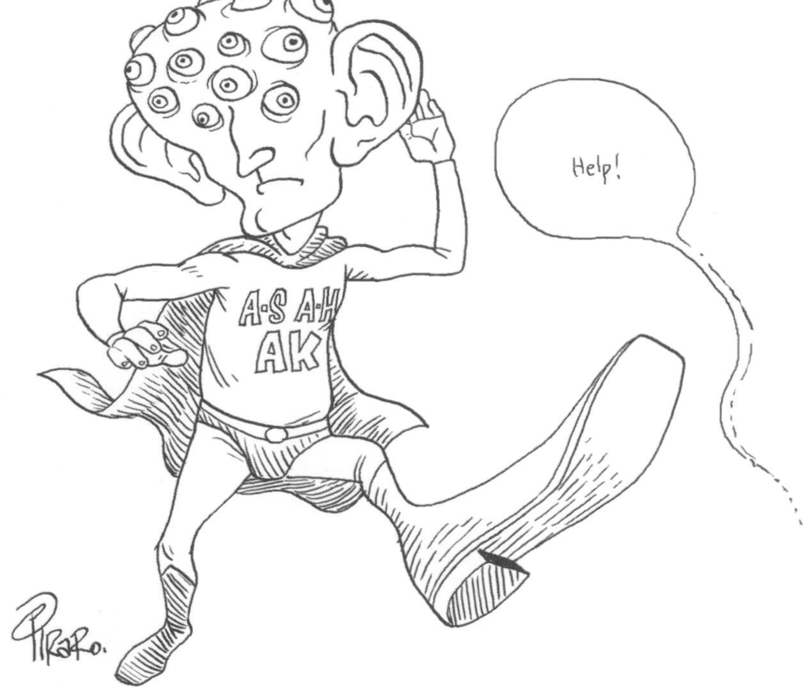
Help!
A·S A·H
AK
PIRARO.

The All-Seeing All-Hearing Ass Kicker

Foreword

When I was a toddler in the early sixties (yes, I'm older than Santa Claus), I watched the original black and white *Superman* show on TV every day. At least, my memory is that it was on every day. The kids in my neighborhood in suburban Kansas City would be out running rampant (before pedophiles, kidnappers, and gang members outnumbered average, forthright citizens)—riding our bikes, petting dogs, chasing popsicle trucks, and pointing up at the sky every time a plane flew over, which was only about every other week. At a certain time each day the front or back doors of most of the houses on the block would open and a woman would poke her head out and shout, "[Boy's name], *Superman* is on!" With kamikaze abandon we would run like hell for our respective houses and hit the floor in front of the refrigerator-sized, wood-paneled TV with a smoky skid of carpet burn.

Sometime around then—I couldn't have been more than four years old—my mom ordered a *Superman* costume for me. I couldn't wait for it to arrive, and when it did my mom and I anxiously tore open the package and unfolded the blue and red miracle within. As she was helping me into it, she noticed some small print on the bottom edge of the shirt that said, "Warning: This suit does not enable the wearer to fly." She read it out loud and laughed, not knowing that inside, a part of me died. I had been certain that this suit would enable me to fly and I was crestfallen to discover it wouldn't. *"What a f*cking ripoff!"* I would have shouted had I been fifteen years older. Instead, I remained silent and didn't show my disappointment.

Once adorned in crime-fighter's garb, I took to the front yard with arms outstretched, running as fast as I could, thinking that perhaps I could prove the warning label wrong. Maybe something magical would happen that clear, sunny day, the kind of thing that happened with absurd regularity in the children's books my parents read to me.

"But this time, as Charlie ran frantically from Old Man Greely's charging Doberman, he lifted off the ground and soared above the treetops."

As I swooped across our front yard, enjoying my make-believe flight as much as I could, an older, much bigger boy approached me. He had a BB gun. "Hey!" the future NRA member shouted. I stopped and stood in front of him, a head shorter and dressed as the Man of Steel. "If you're Superman, then you can stop bullets," the lunk spat in his deep, raspy, sarcastic, eight-year-old voice. When he pointed the BB gun at me to test his theory, I turned and ran frantically for the front door of my house. That dash to safety was the closest I would ever come to flying in that suit.

Once safely inside, I felt a sting on the back of my thigh where I had been shot. Terrified, I ran to my room, took off the suit, and never wore it outside the house again.

This kind of incident is not uncommon in the life of a young boy, and I think it is one of the reasons that super heroes are so appealing. How cool would it have been to be able to grab that BB gun out of that kid's hands and tie it into a big, metal pretzel? Revenge scenarios like that played in my head for years: grabbing him by the collar as I flew into the air and dropping him onto the roof of the police station; punching him in the jaw and bending his rifle around his neck as he lay unconscious; flying counterclockwise around the earth fast enough to turn back time and smothering him in his crib at the hospital.

Though I've long since forgiven the gun-wielding hun of my Kansas City neighborhood, I still yearn for super powers. With invisibility I could expose the unethical behavior of politicians (and sneak into

Penelope Cruz's bedroom). With the ability to fly I could avoid the security lines at airports (and hover outside the window of Penelope Cruz's bedroom). With superhuman strength I could foil robberies (and escape the clutches of Penelope Cruz's security team). And that's only the traditional, garden-variety powers. Imagine what you could do with telekinesis, time travel, shape shifting, clairvoyance, or the ability to find your car keys and the TV remote no matter where they are hiding.

But since these powers are beyond my mortal reach (you're safe, Penelope), I content myself with being able to make people laugh, which in itself is a pretty cool thing. I hope you get a chuckle or two from this book, and if you ever see a picture in a magazine of me and Penelope Cruz on a date, you'll know I've been granted some kind of yet unnamed super power.

Dan Piraro, May 2010

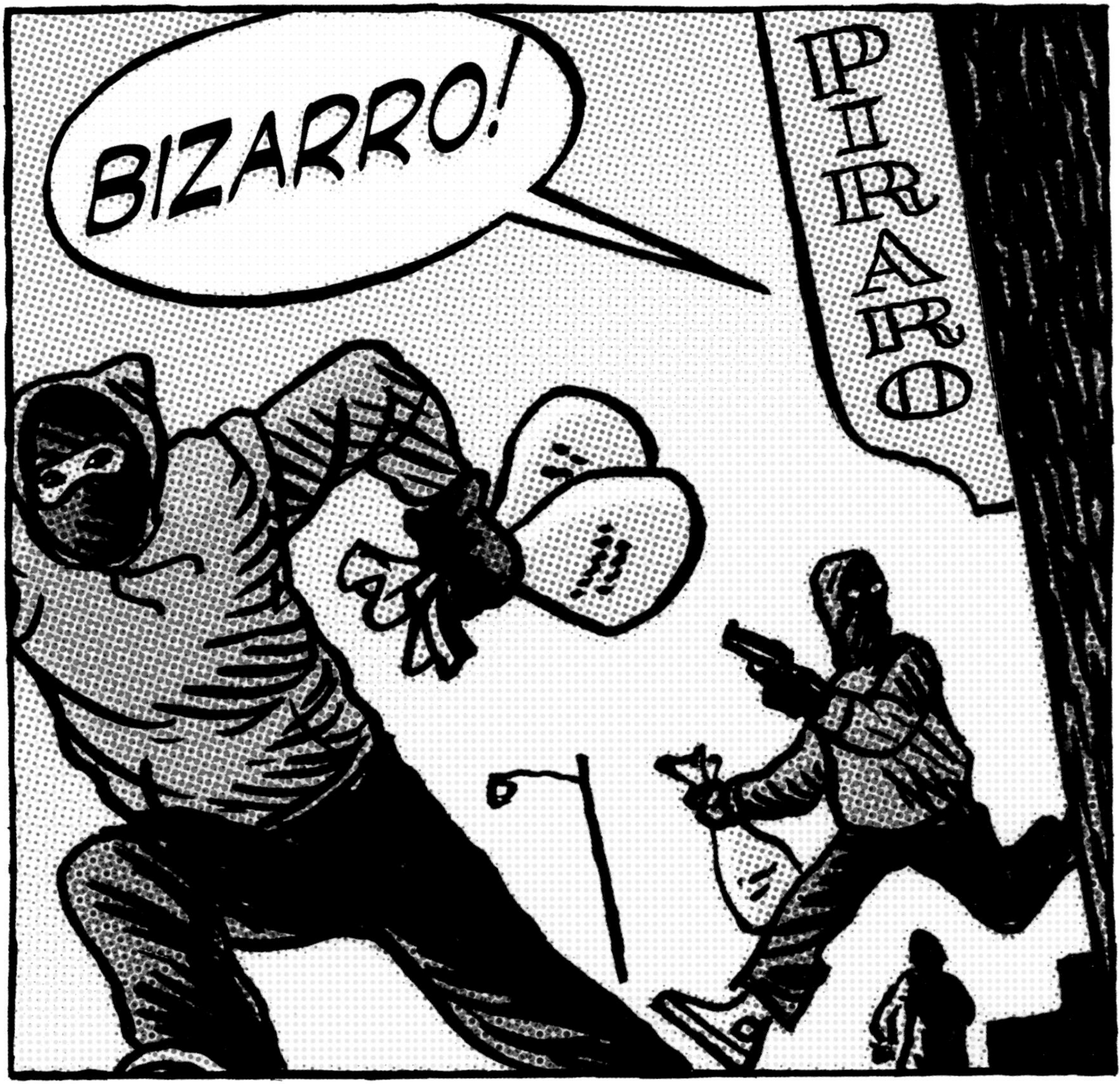
BIZARRO!
PIRARO

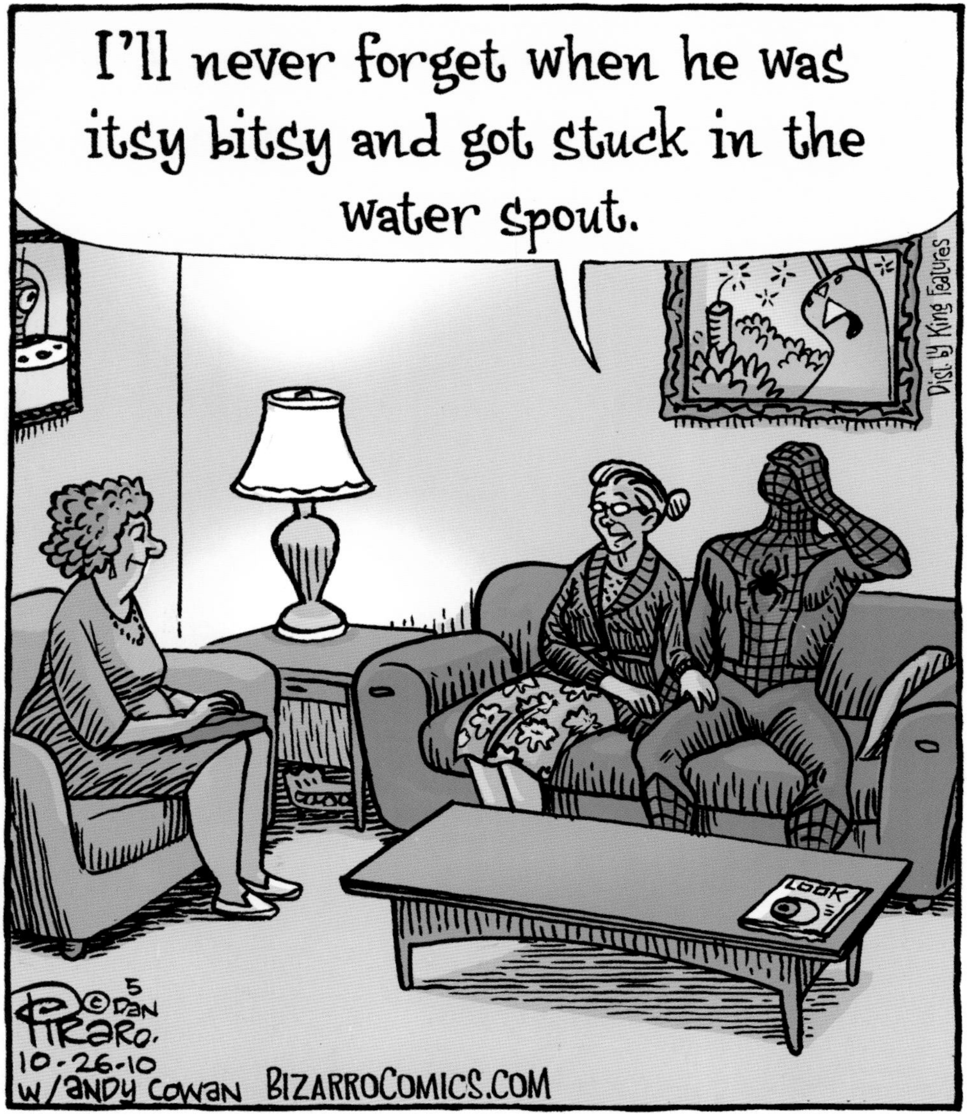
I'll never forget when he was itsy bitsy and got stuck in the water spout.
Dist. by King Features
LOOK
© DAN PIRARO 10-26-10
w/ANDY COWAN BIZARROCOMICS.COM

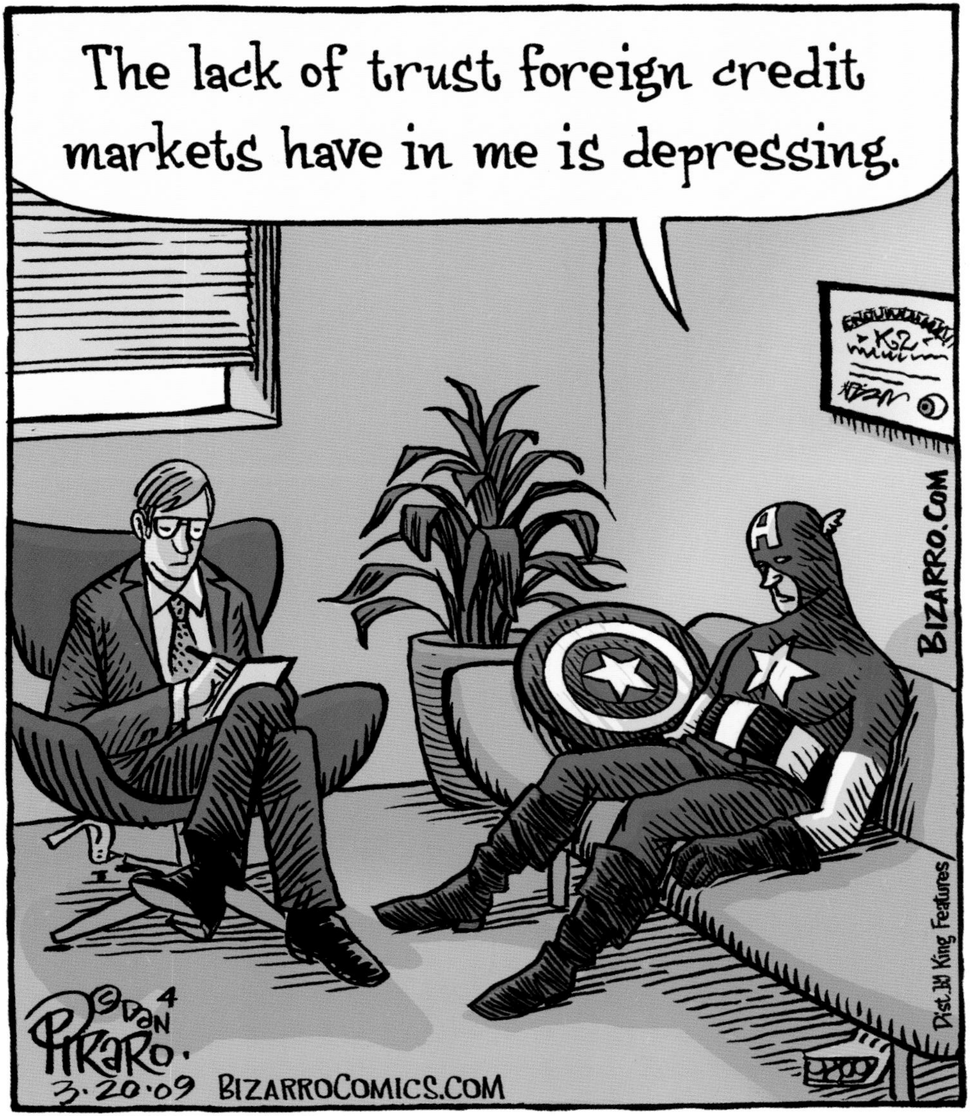
The lack of trust foreign credit markets have in me is depressing.
BIZARRO.COM
Dist. by King Features
DAN PIRARO
3.20.09 BIZARROCOMICS.COM

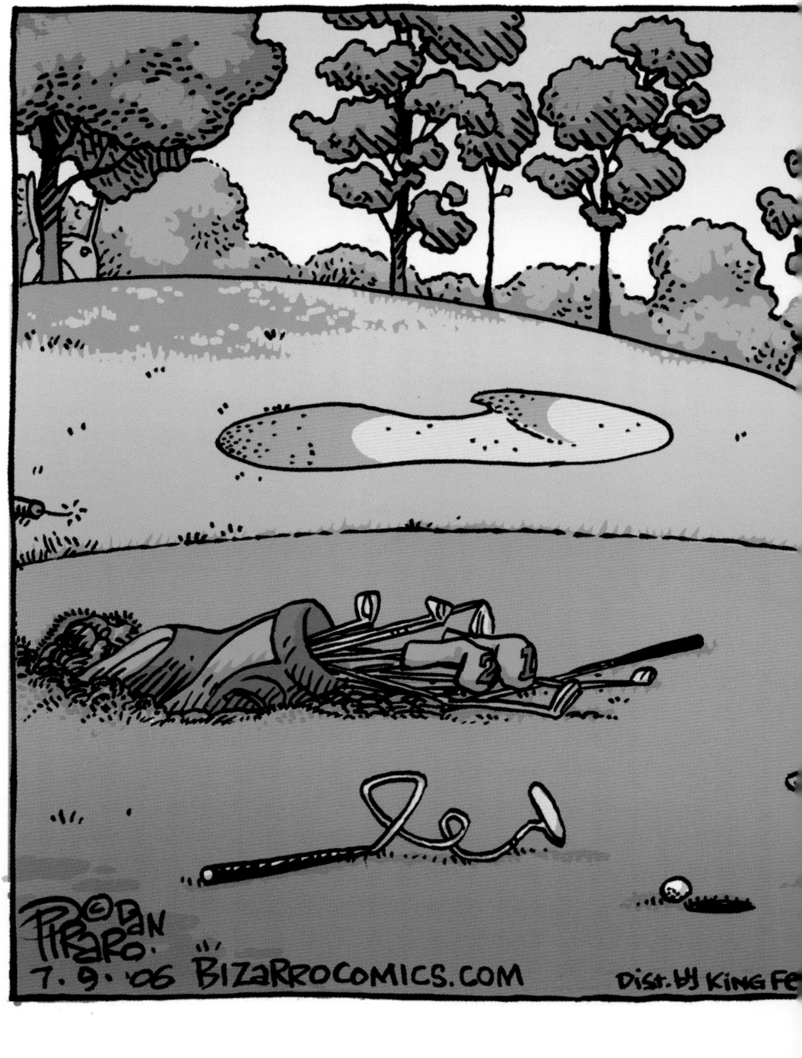

2
1
©DAN PIRARO
7.9.'06 BIZARROCOMICS.COM
Dist. by King Fe

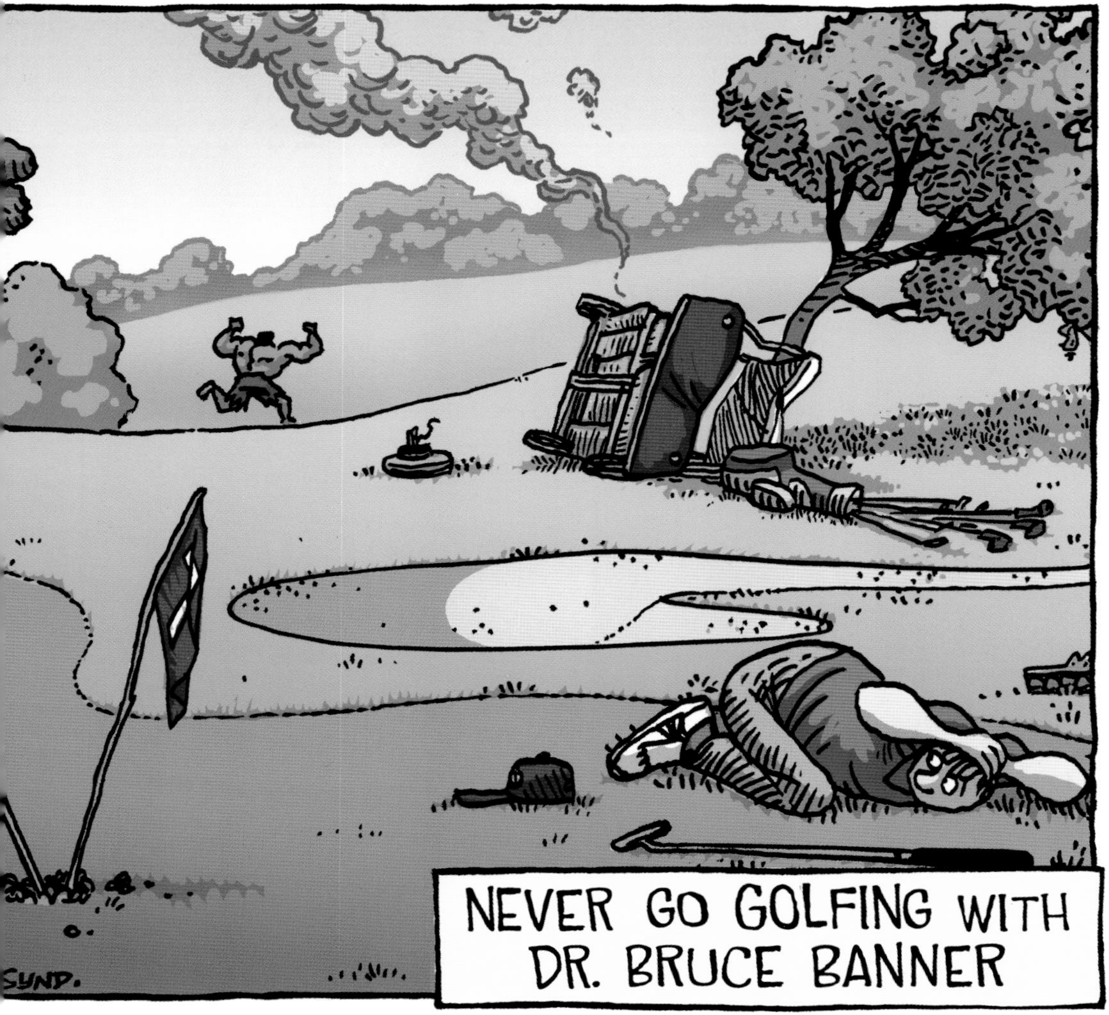
NEVER GO GOLFING WITH DR. BRUCE BANNER
SUND.

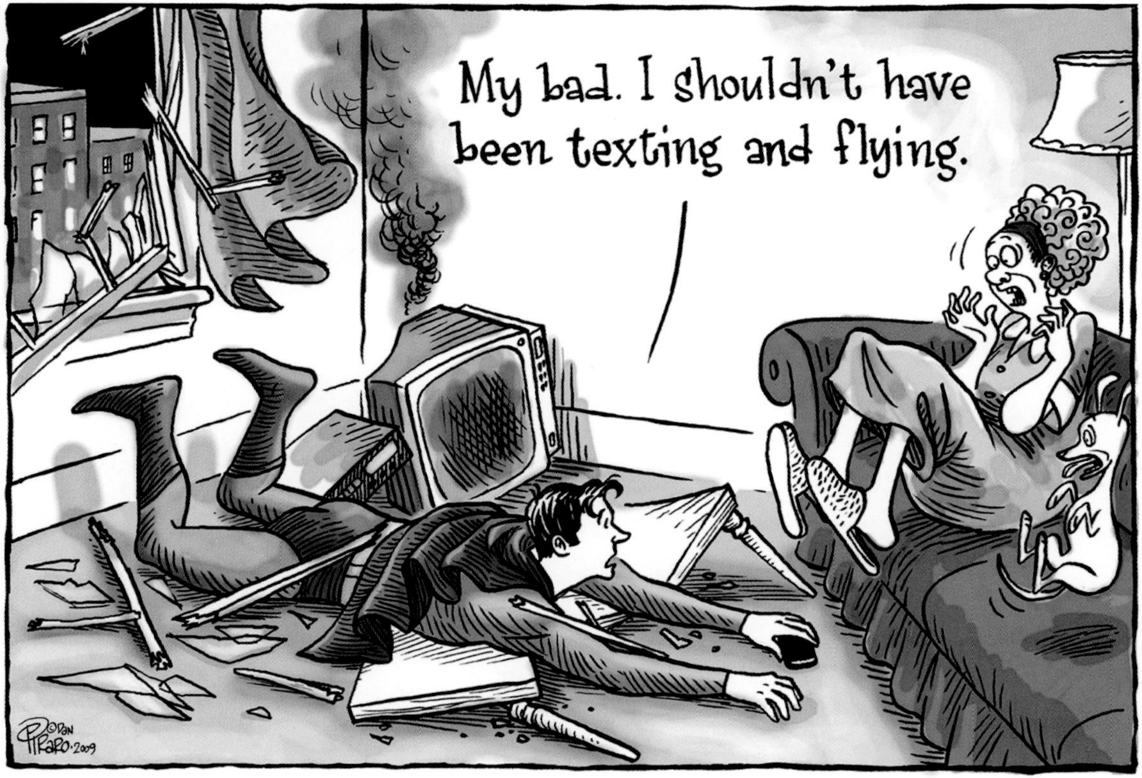
My bad. I shouldn't have been texting and flying.
©DAN PIRARO·2009

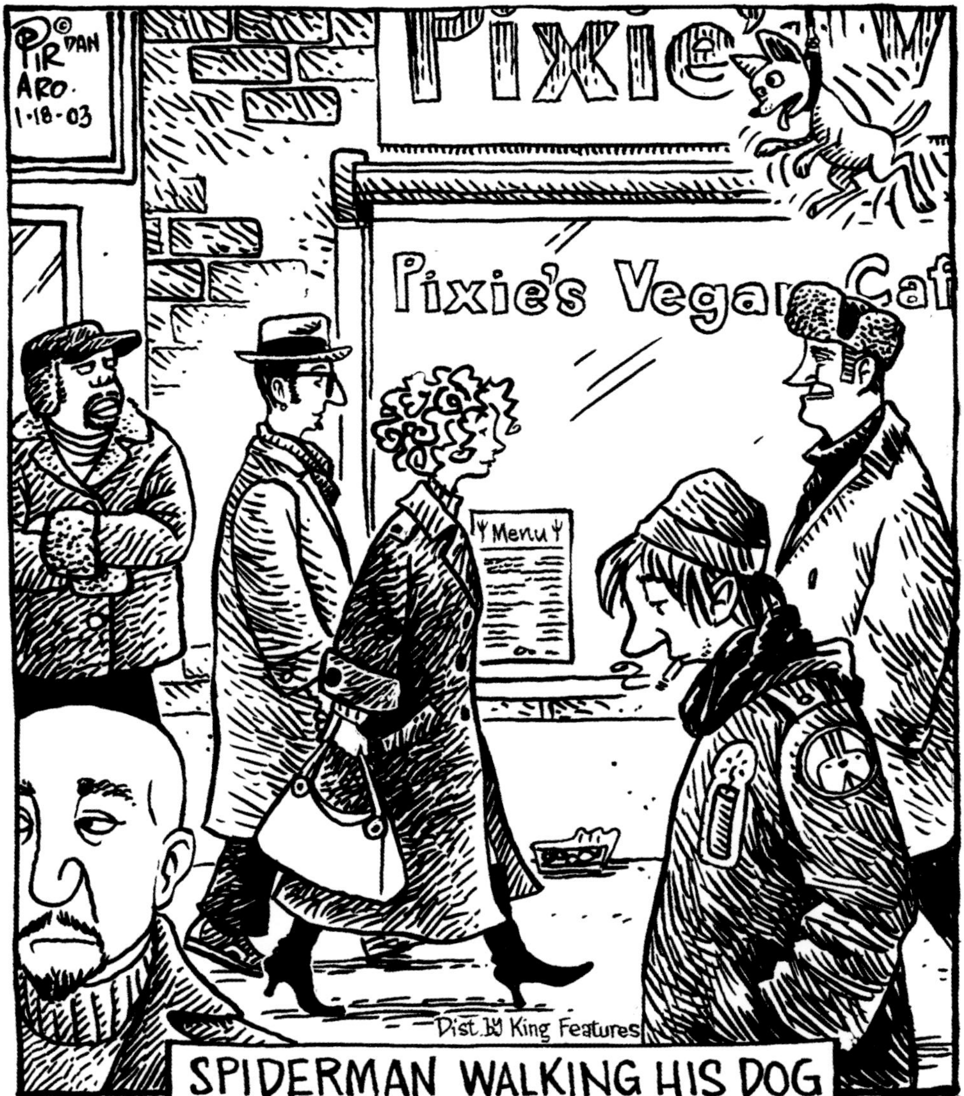

© DAN PIRARO 1-18-03
Pixie's
Pixie's Vegan Caf
Menu
Dist. by King Features
SPIDERMAN WALKING HIS DOG

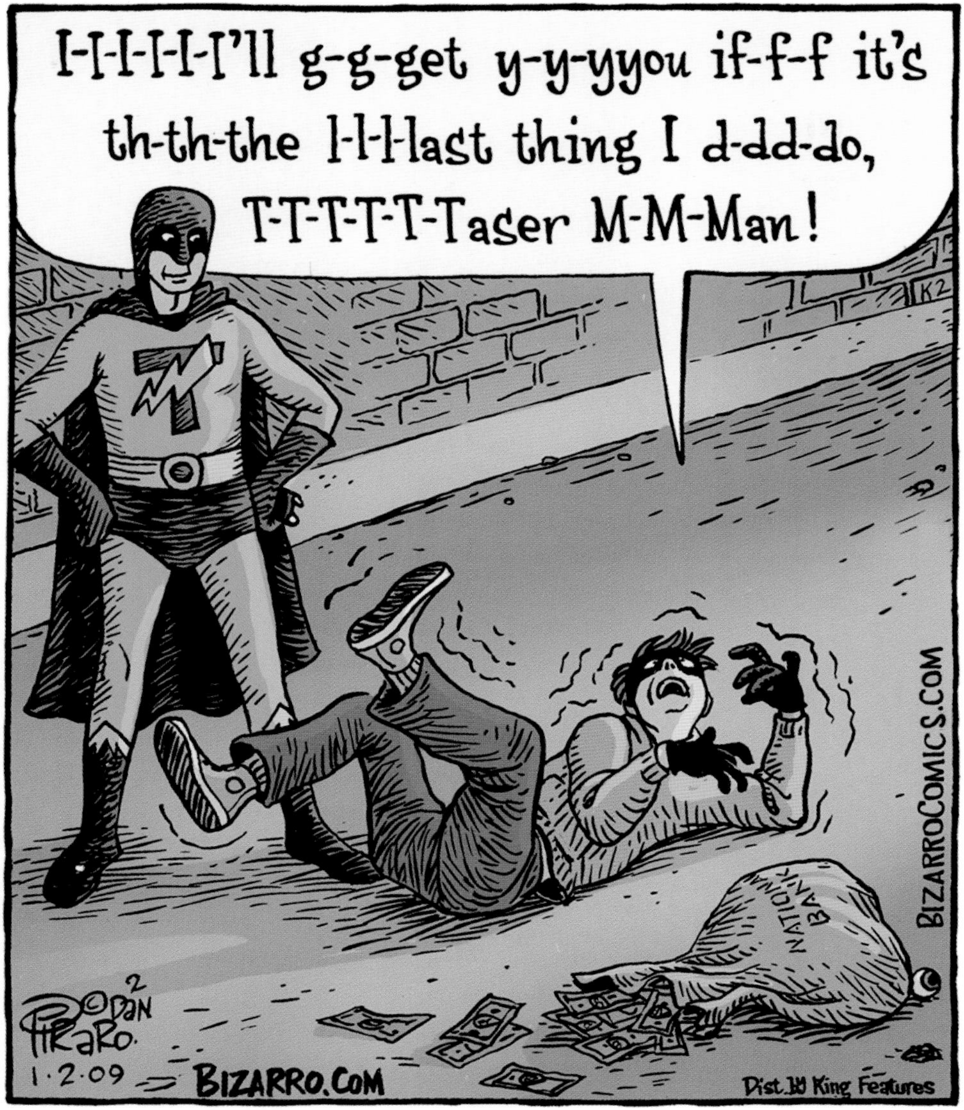
I-I-I-I-I-I'll g-g-get y-y-yyou if-f-f it's th-th-the l-l-l-last thing I d-dd-do, T-T-T-T-T-Taser M-M-Man!
NATIONAL BANK
©DAN PIRARO 1·2·09
BIZARRO.COM
BIZARROCOMICS.COM
Dist. by King Features

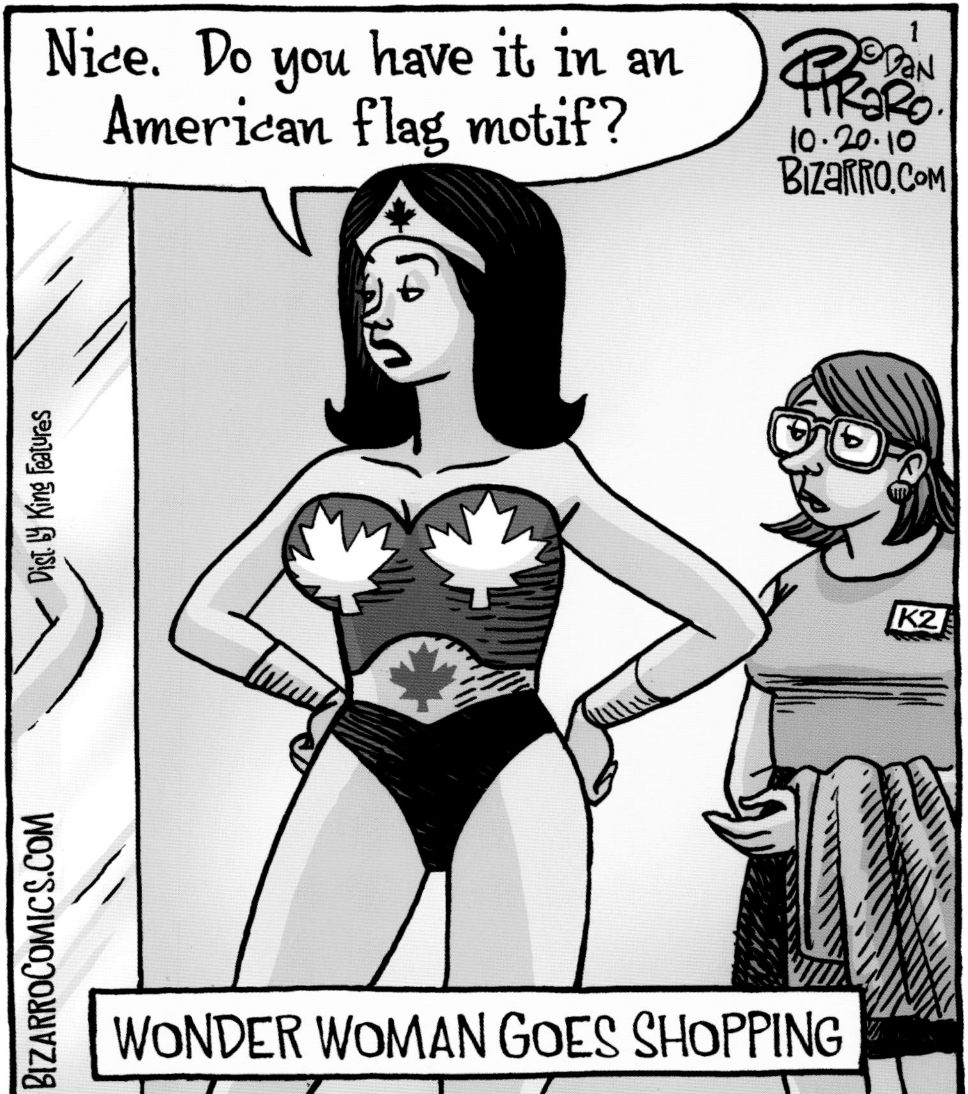
Nice. Do you have it in an American flag motif?
©DAN PIRARO. 10·20·10 BIZARRO.COM
Dist. by King Features
BIZARROCOMICS.COM
K2
WONDER WOMAN GOES SHOPPING

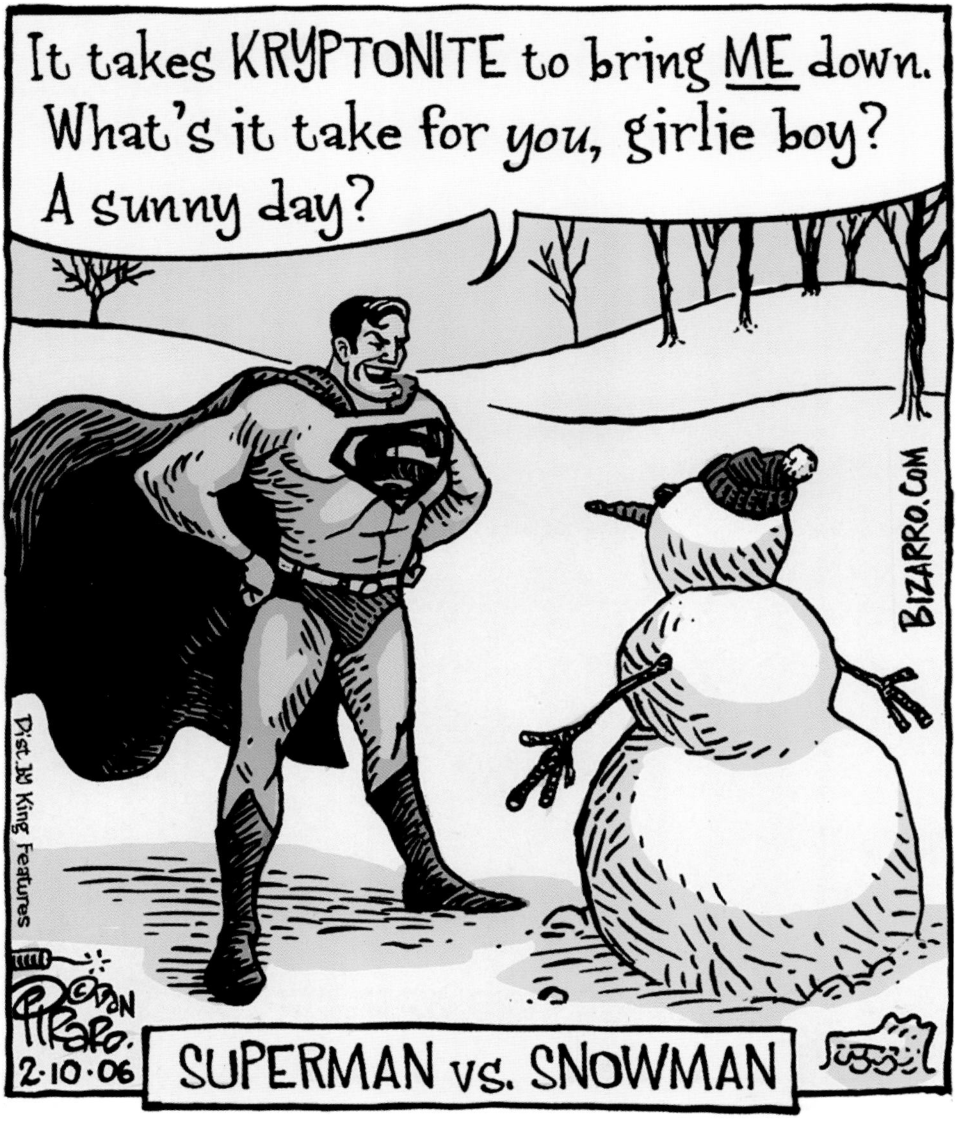
It takes KRYPTONITE to bring ME down. What's it take for you, girlie boy? A sunny day?
BIZARRO.COM
Dist. by King Features
© Dan Piraro. 2.10.06
SUPERMAN vs. SNOWMAN

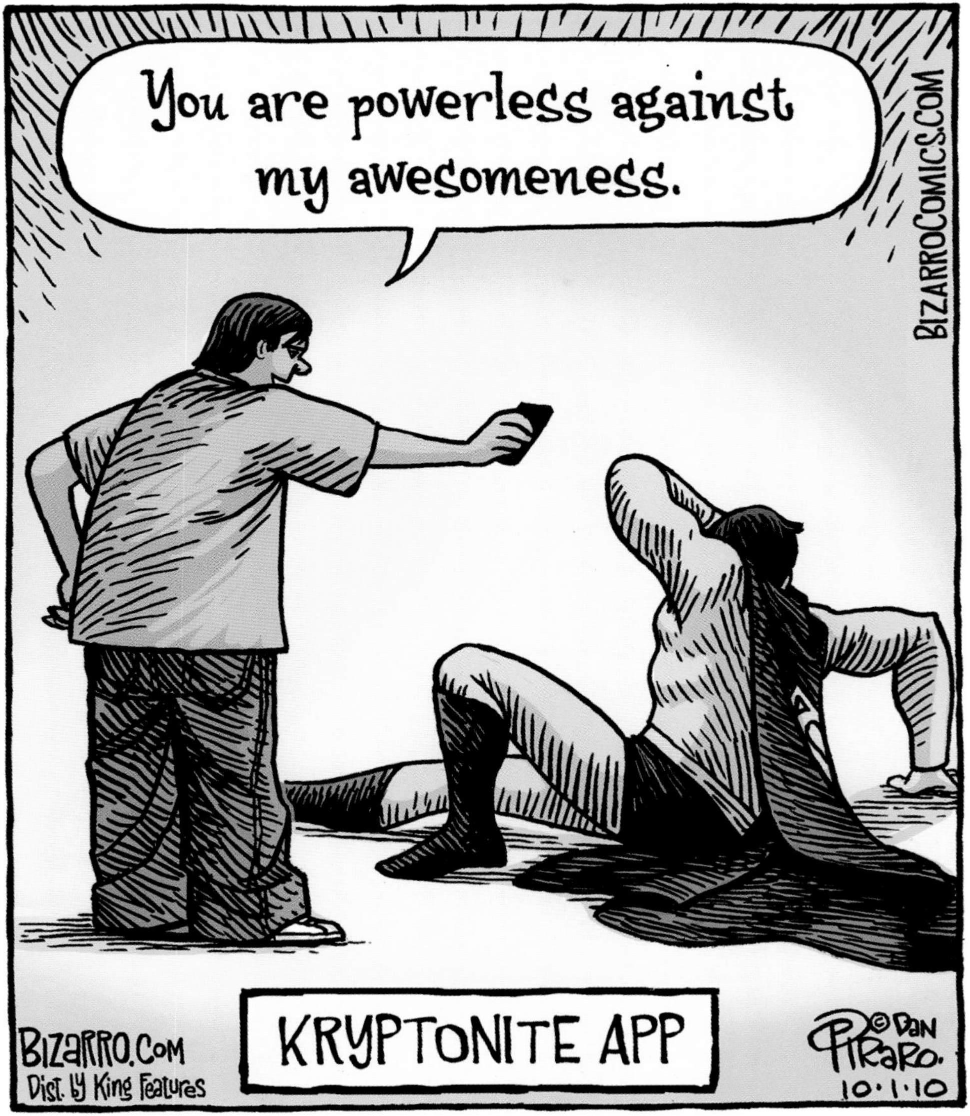

You are powerless against my awesomeness.
BIZARROCOMICS.COM
BIZARRO.COM
Dist. by King Features
KRYPTONITE APP
© DAN PIRARO.
10·1·10

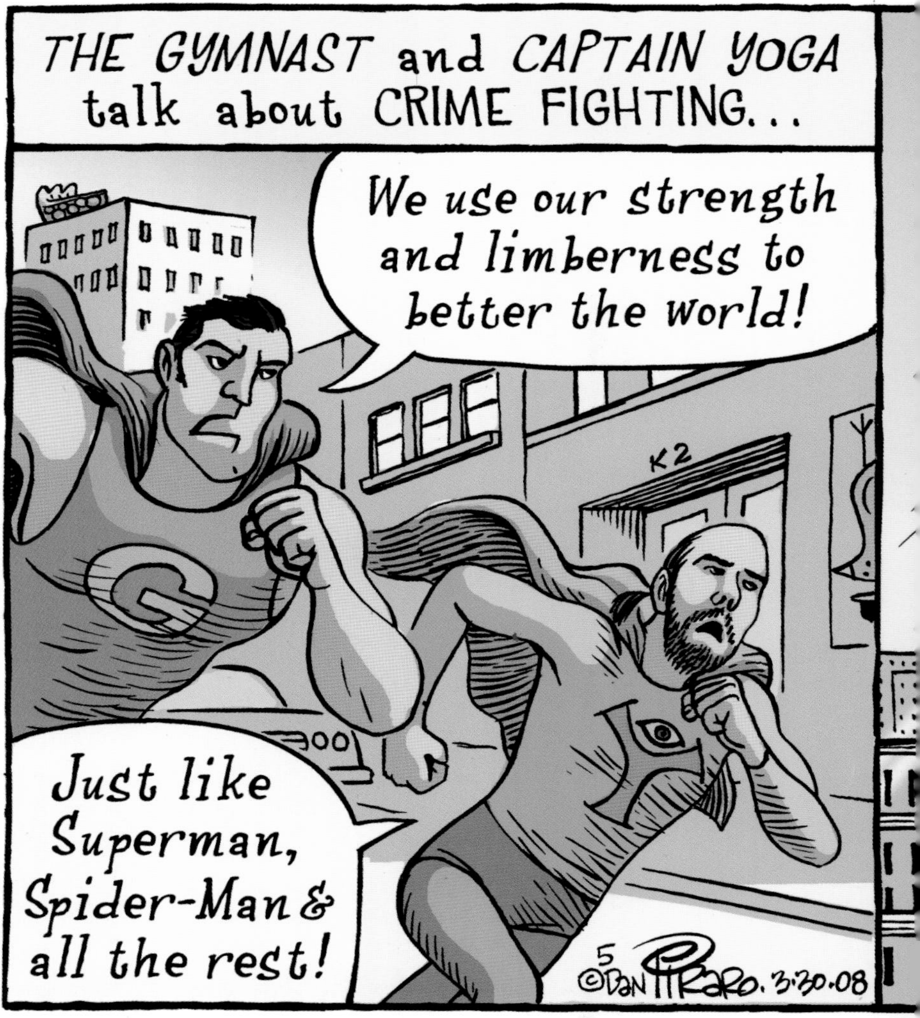
THE GYMNAST and CAPTAIN YOGA talk about CRIME FIGHTING...
We use our strength and limberness to better the world!
Just like Superman, Spider-Man & all the rest!
K2
©DAN PIRARO. 3.30.08

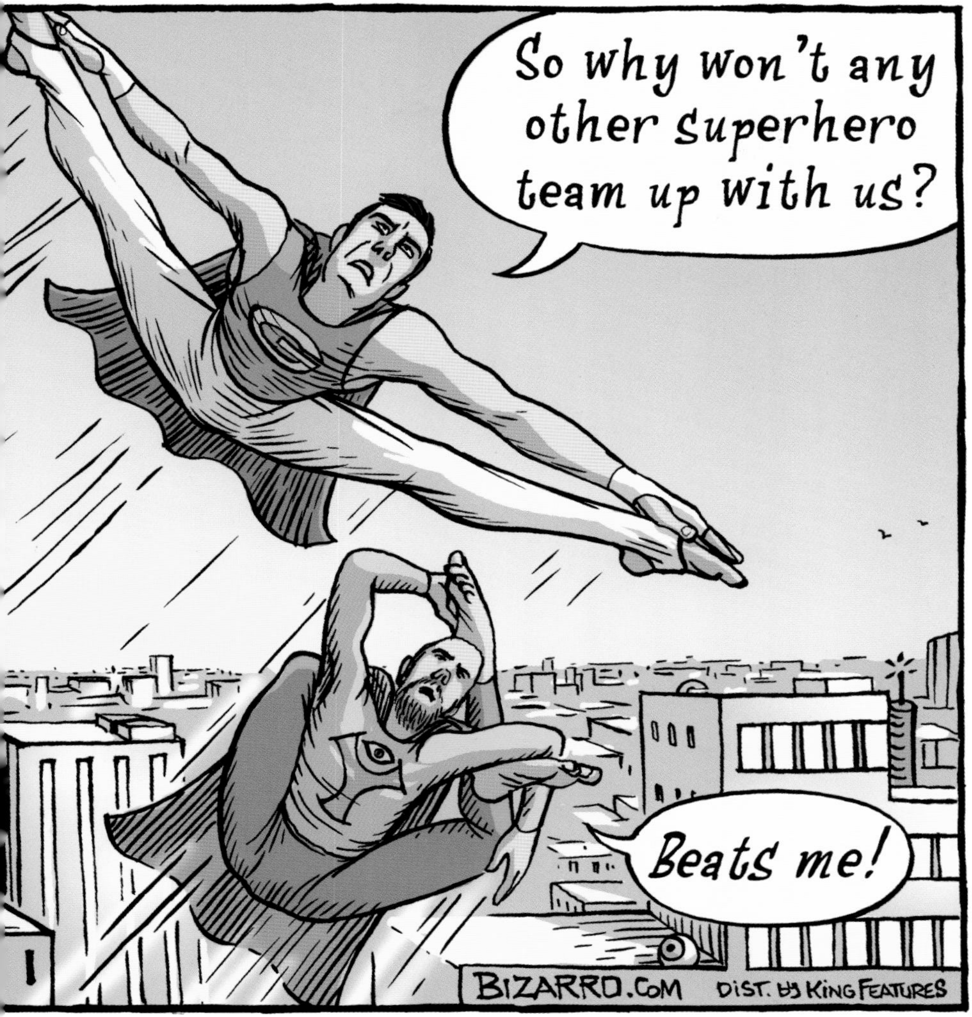
So why won't any other superhero team up with us?
Beats me!
BIZARRO.COM
DIST. BY KING FEATURES

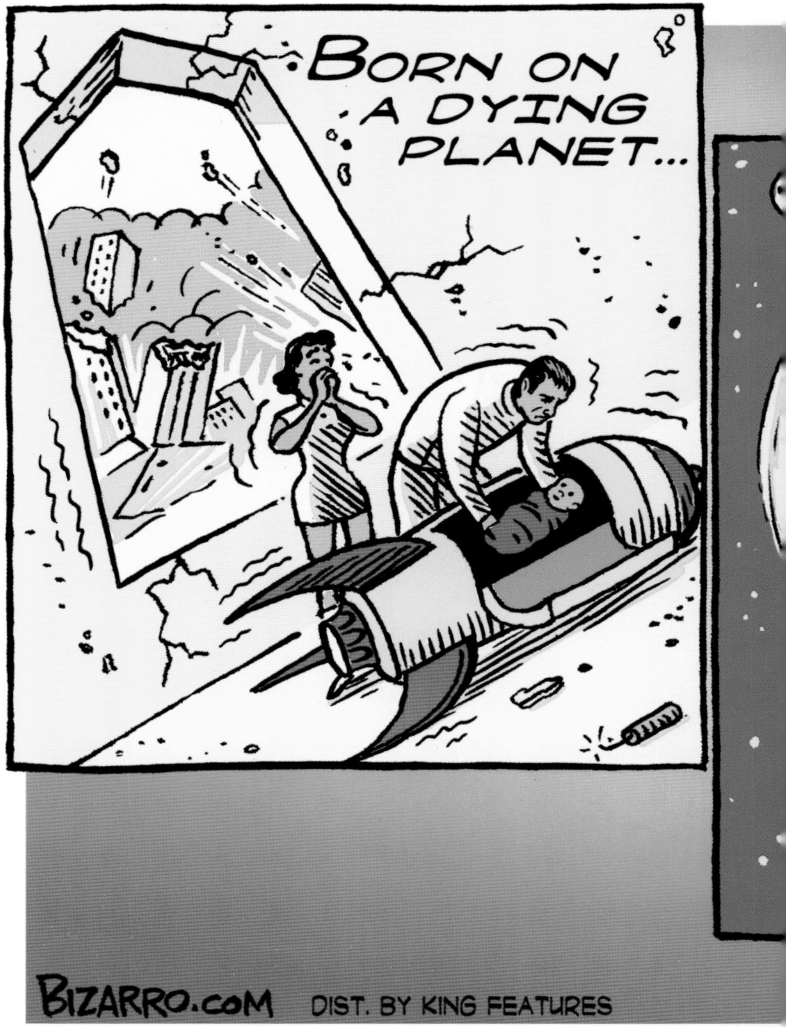

BORN ON A DYING PLANET...
BIZARRO.COM
DIST. BY KING FEATURES

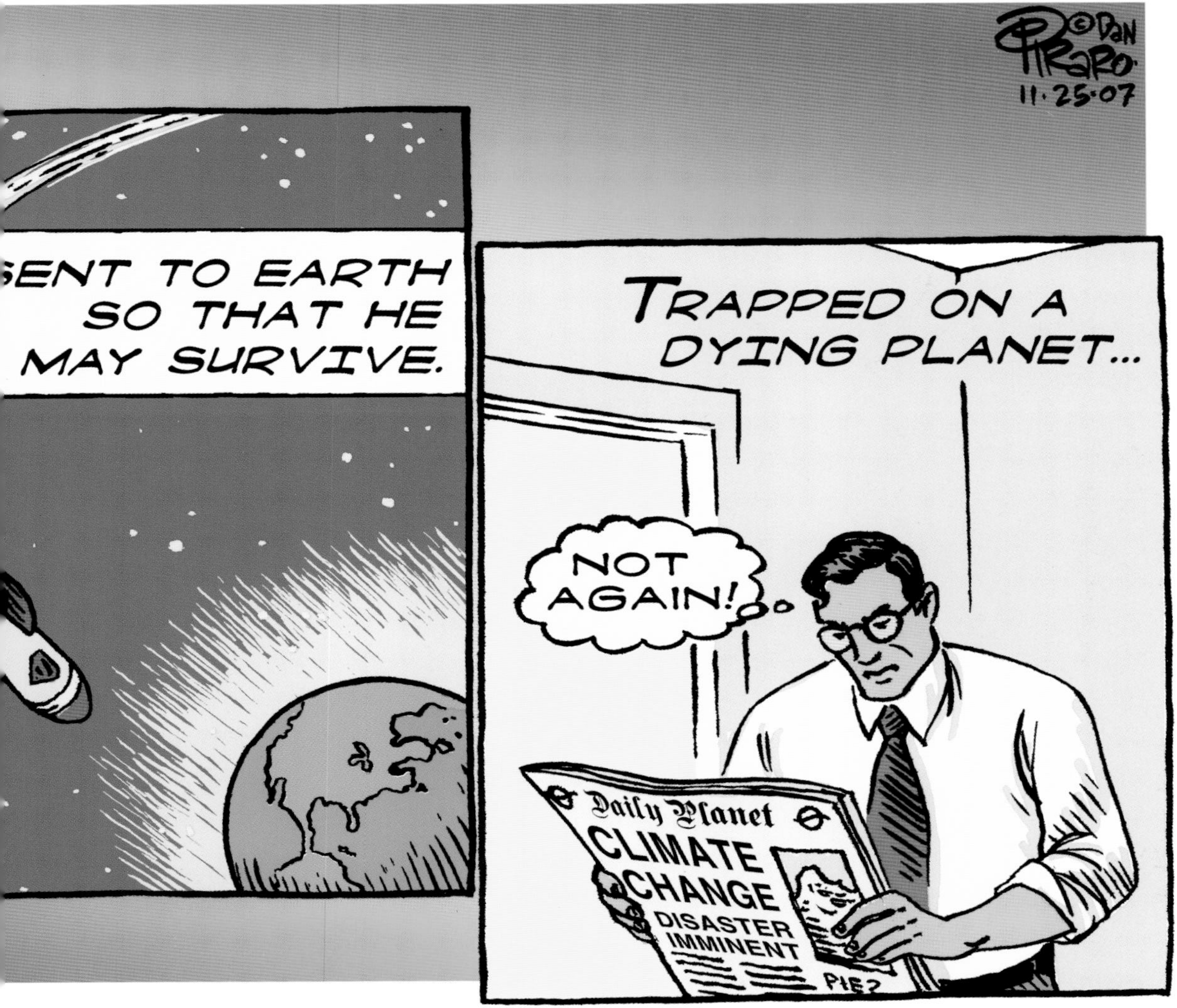
©DAN PIRARO 11·25·07
SENT TO EARTH SO THAT HE MAY SURVIVE.
TRAPPED ON A DYING PLANET...
NOT AGAIN!
Daily Planet
CLIMATE CHANGE
DISASTER IMMINENT

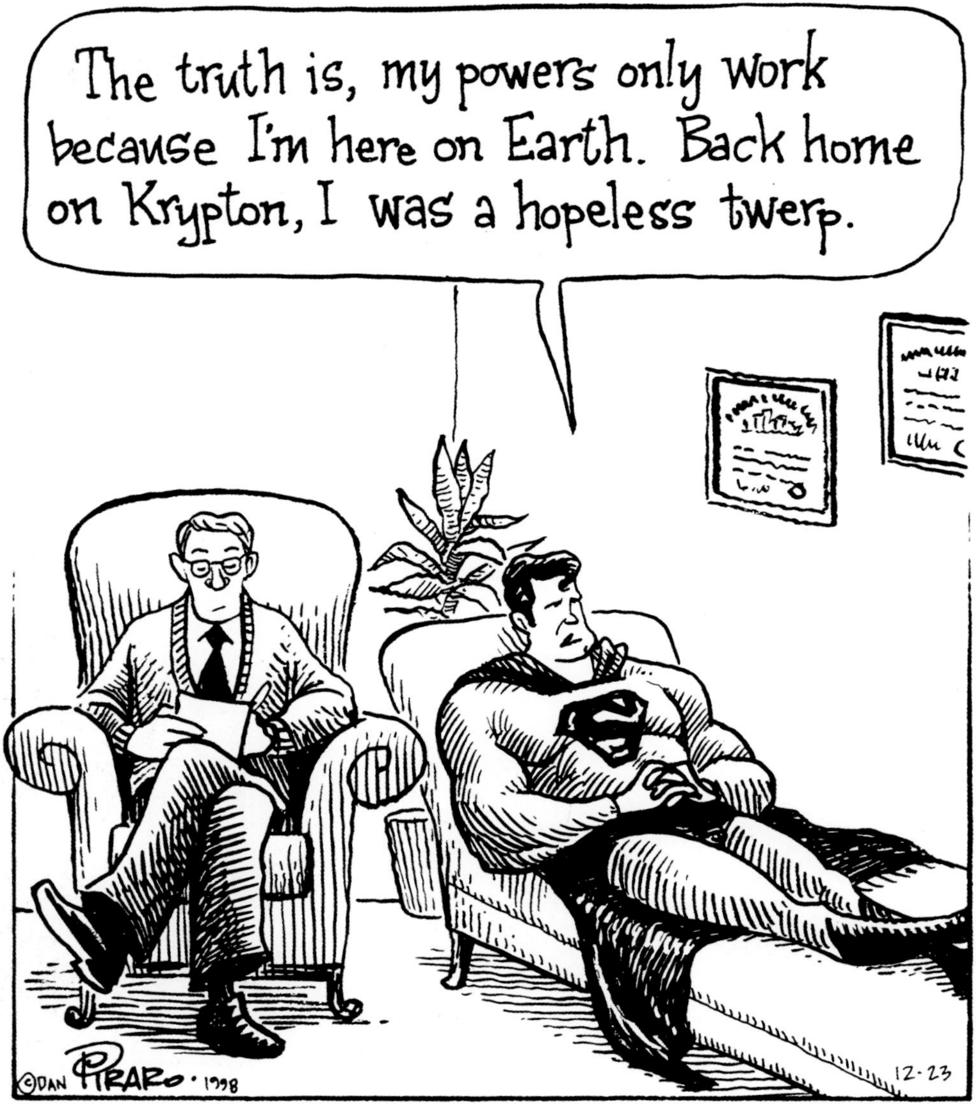
The truth is, my powers only work because I'm here on Earth. Back home on Krypton, I was a hopeless twerp.
©DAN PIRARO · 1998
12-23

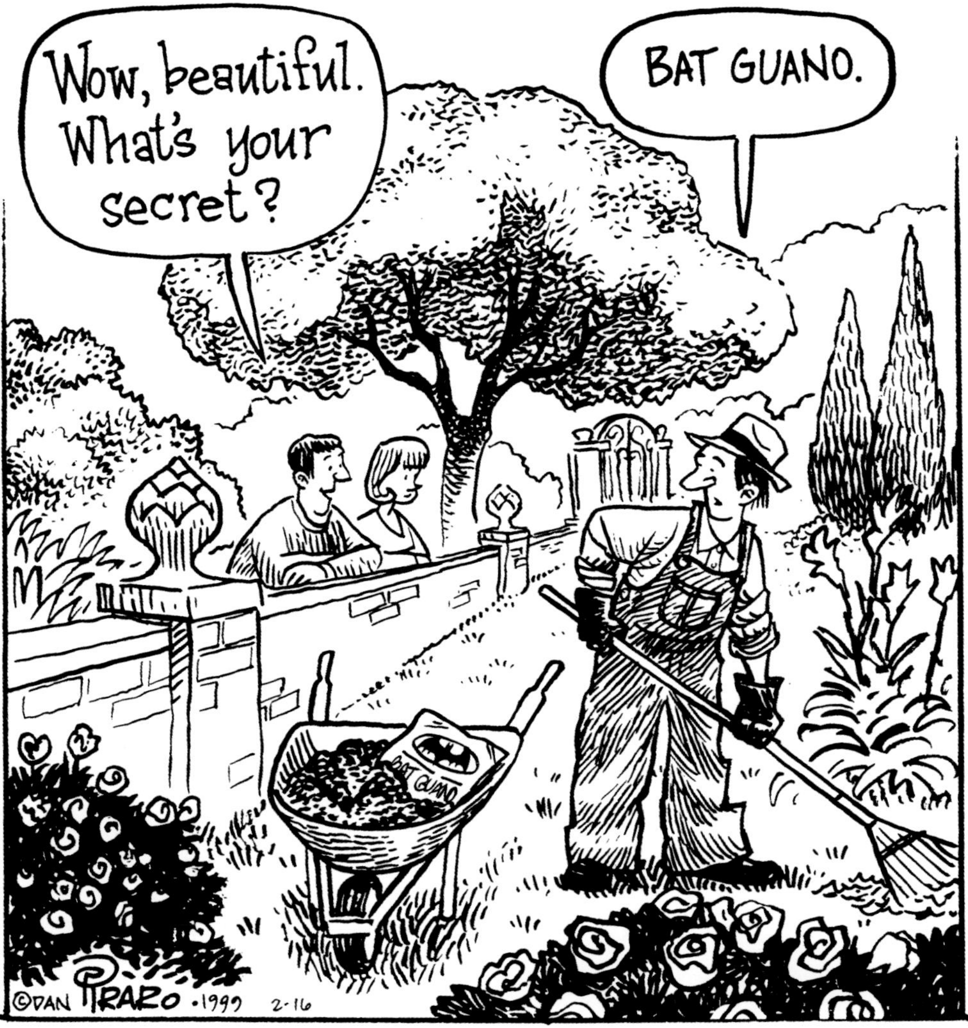
Wow, beautiful. What's your secret?
BAT GUANO.
BAT GUANO
©DAN PIRARO ·1999 2-16

THE LEGENDARY GARDENS OF WAYNE MANOR

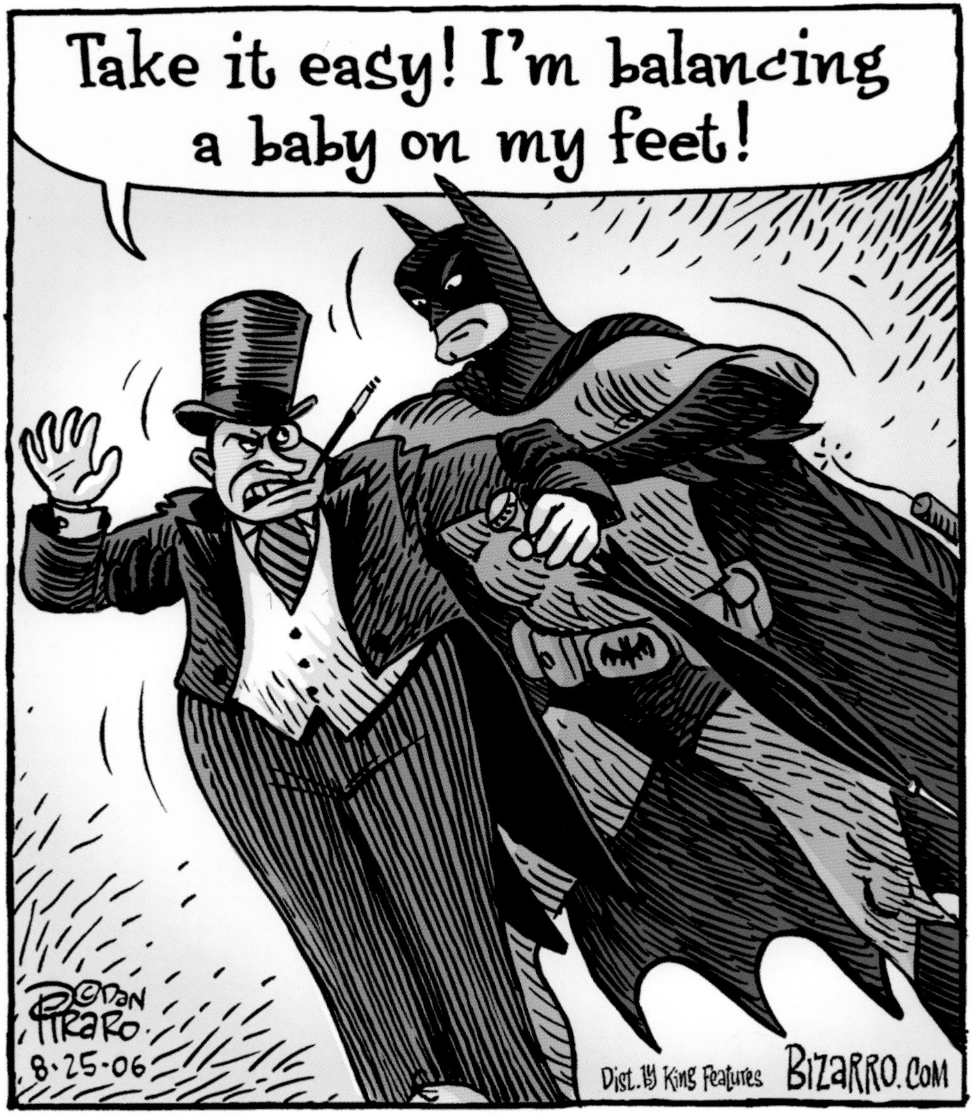
Take it easy! I'm balancing a baby on my feet!
©Dan Piraro 8-25-06
Dist. by King Features
BIZARRO.COM

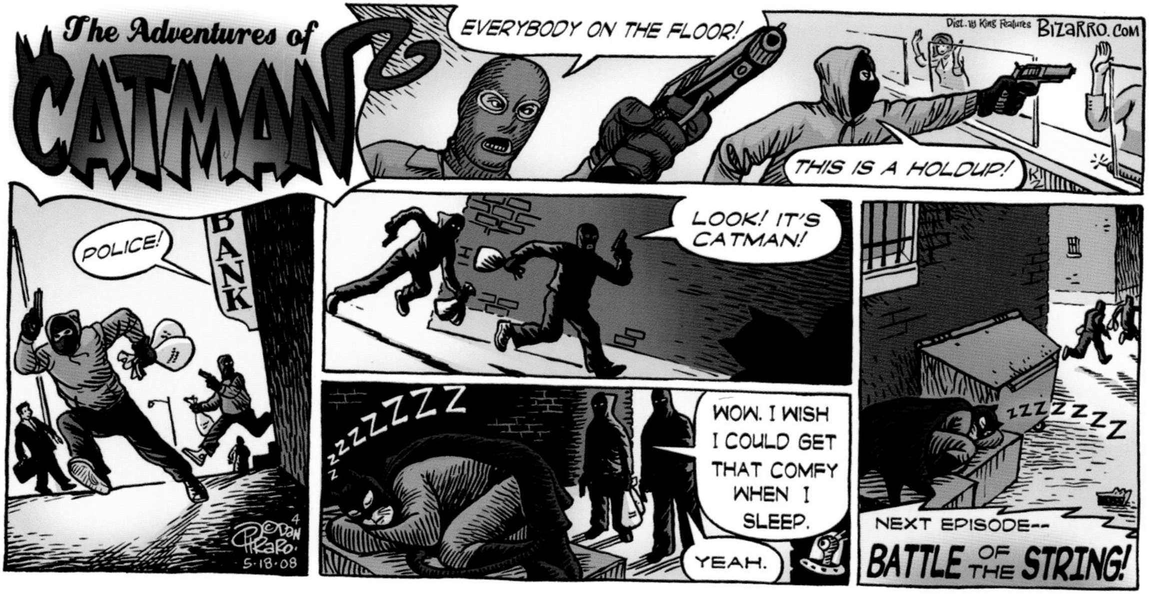
The Adventures of
CATMAN
Dist. by King Features BIZARRO.COM
EVERYBODY ON THE FLOOR!
THIS IS A HOLDUP!
POLICE!
BANK
LOOK! IT'S CATMAN!
ZZZZZZZ
WOW. I WISH I COULD GET THAT COMFY WHEN I SLEEP.
YEAH.
ZZZZZZZ
NEXT EPISODE--
BATTLE OF THE STRING!
©DAN PIRARO 5·18·08

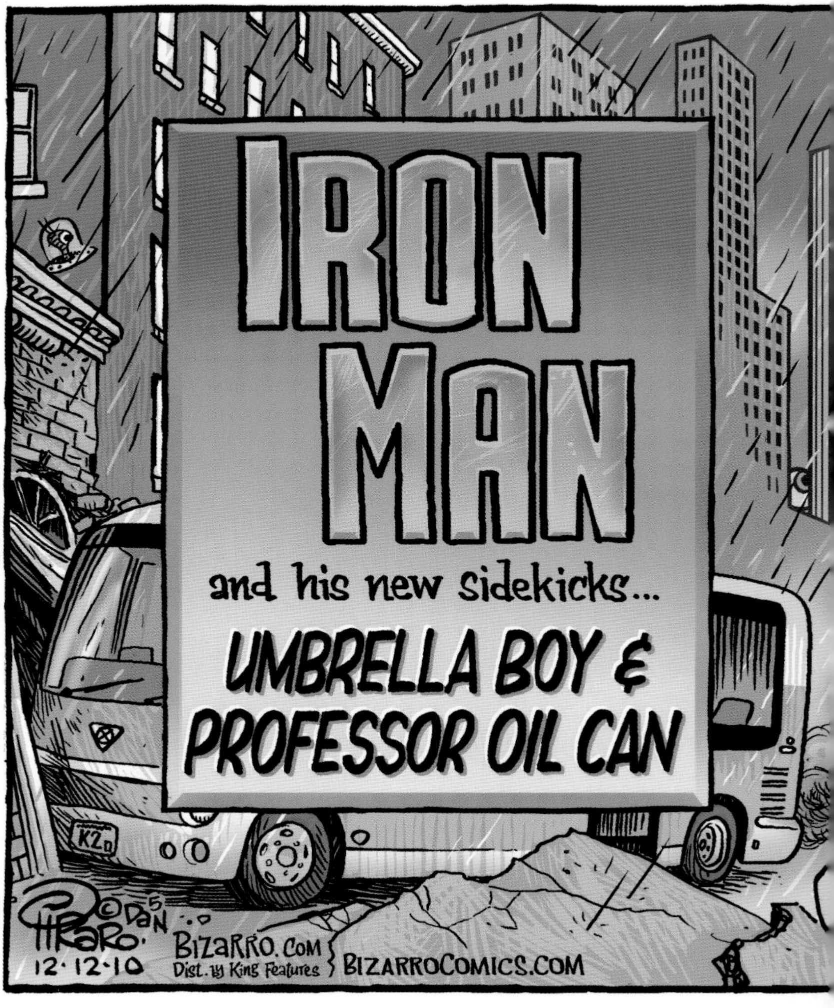
IRON MAN
and his new sidekicks...
UMBRELLA BOY &
PROFESSOR OIL CAN
K2
©DAN PIRARO
12·12·10
BIZARRO.COM
Dist. by King Features
BIZARROCOMICS.COM

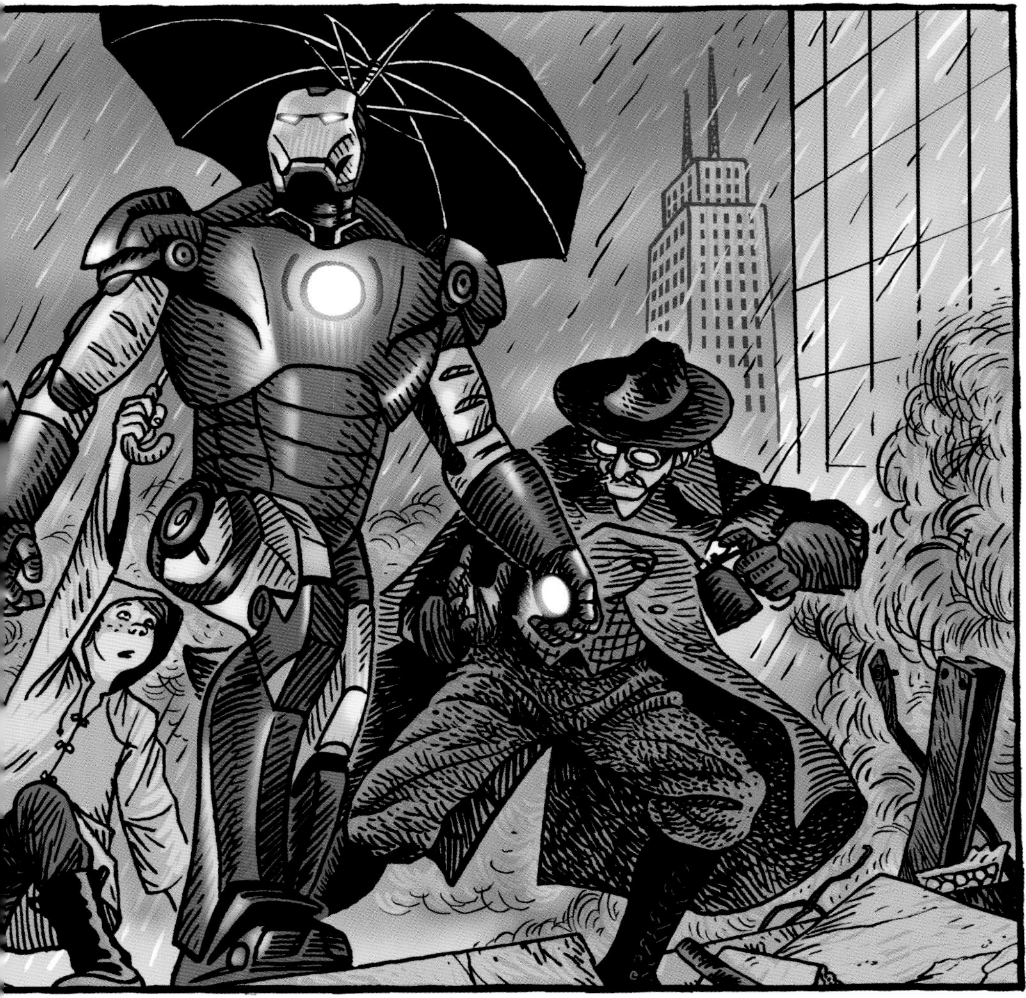

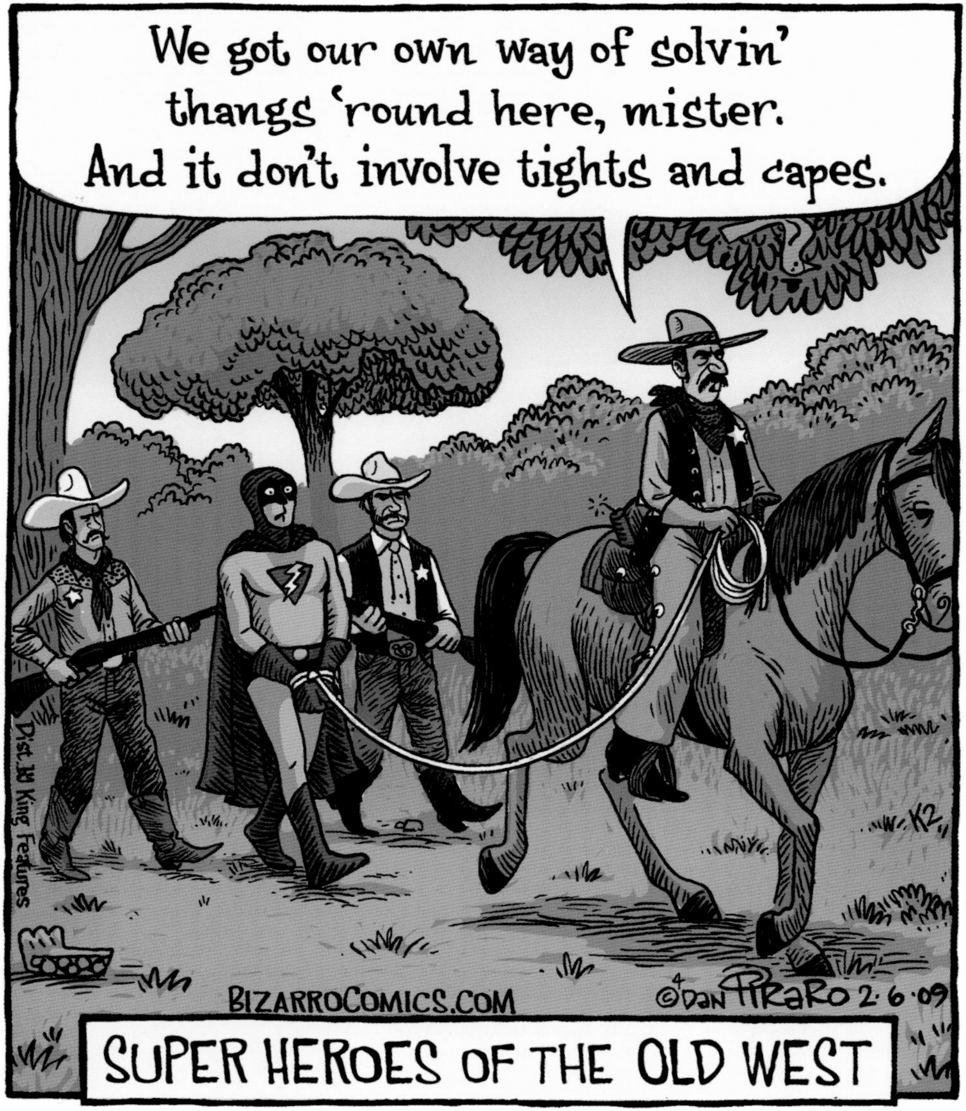
We got our own way of solvin' thangs 'round here, mister. And it don't involve tights and capes.
Dist. by King Features
BIZARROCOMICS.COM
© DAN PIRARO 2·6·09
SUPER HEROES OF THE OLD WEST

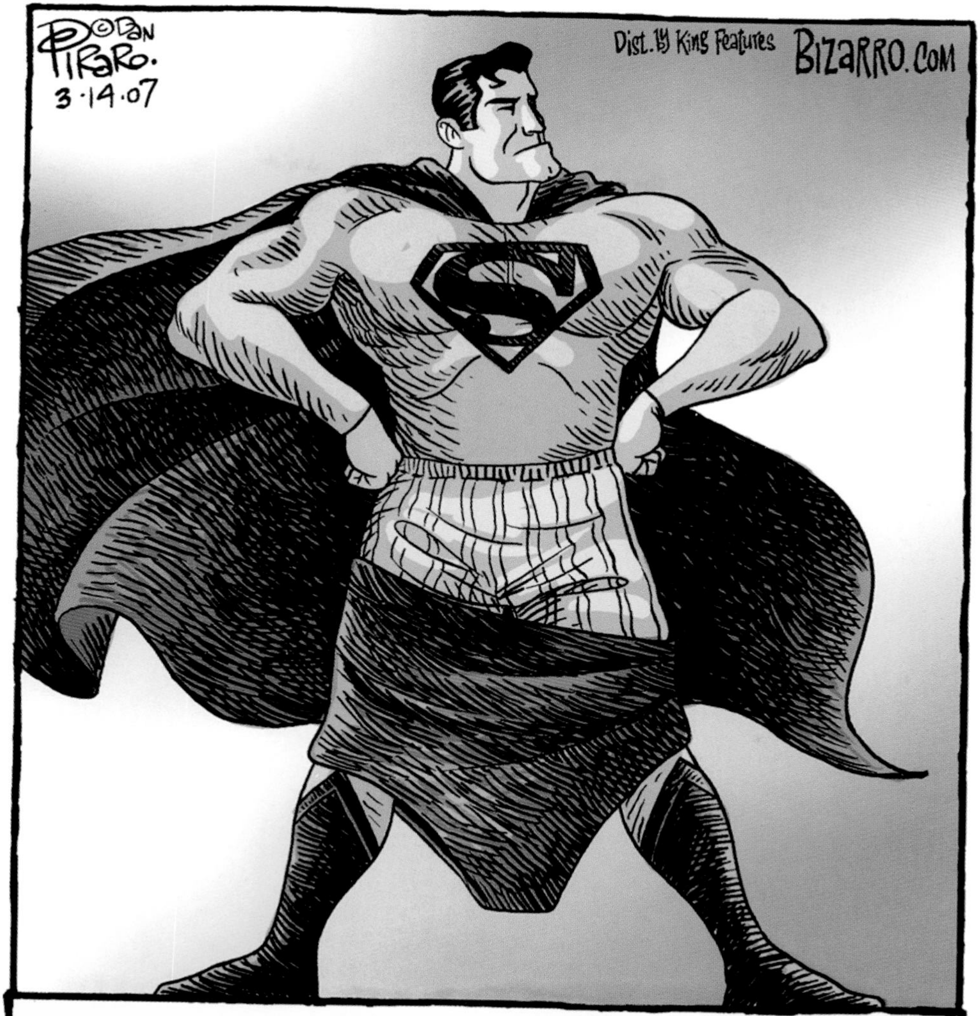
©Dan Piraro. 3·14·07
Dist. by King Features
Bizarro.com

THE MAN OF STEEL GIVES IN TO FASHION

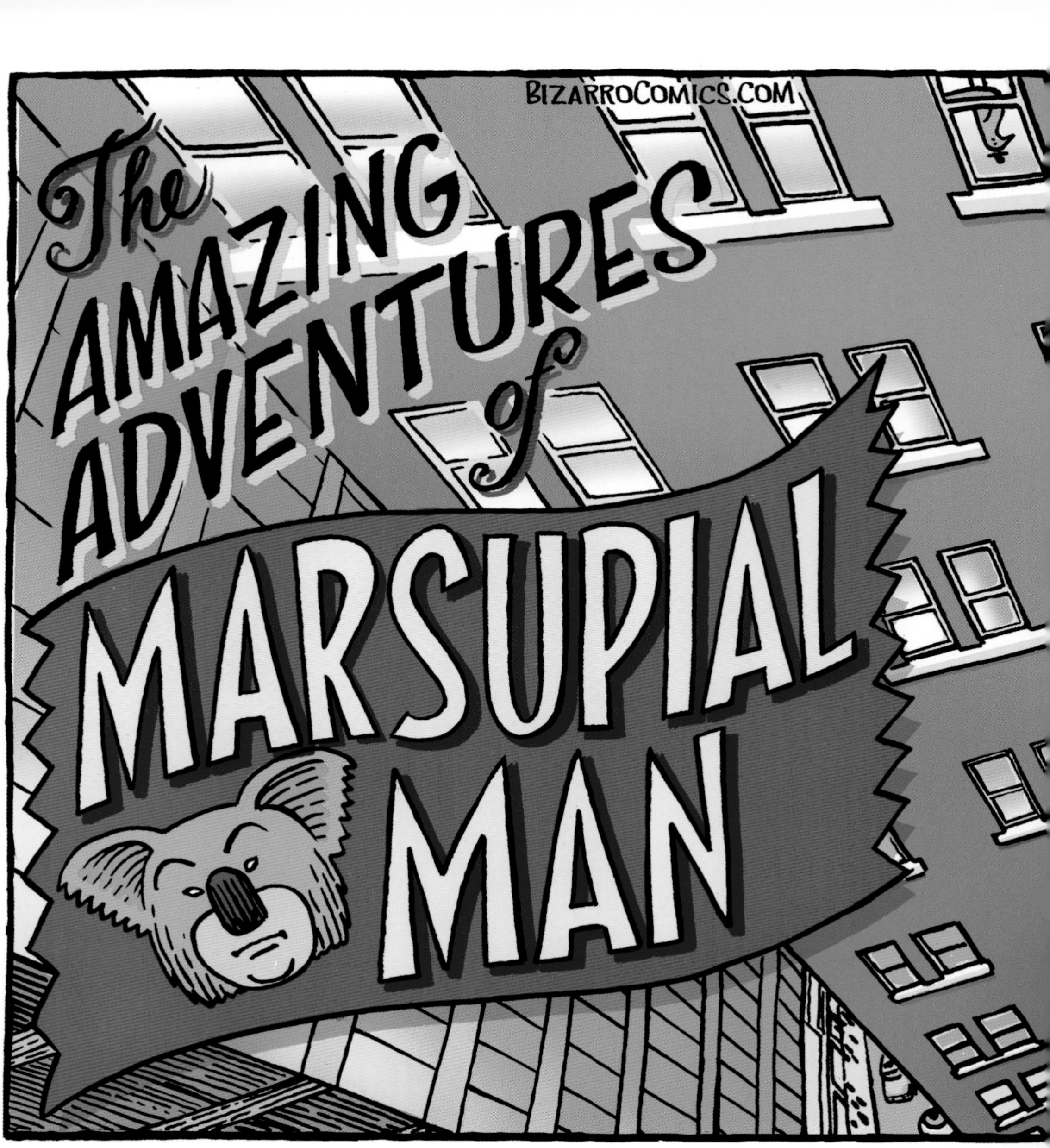
BIZARROCOMICS.COM
The AMAZING ADVENTURES of
MARSUPIAL MAN

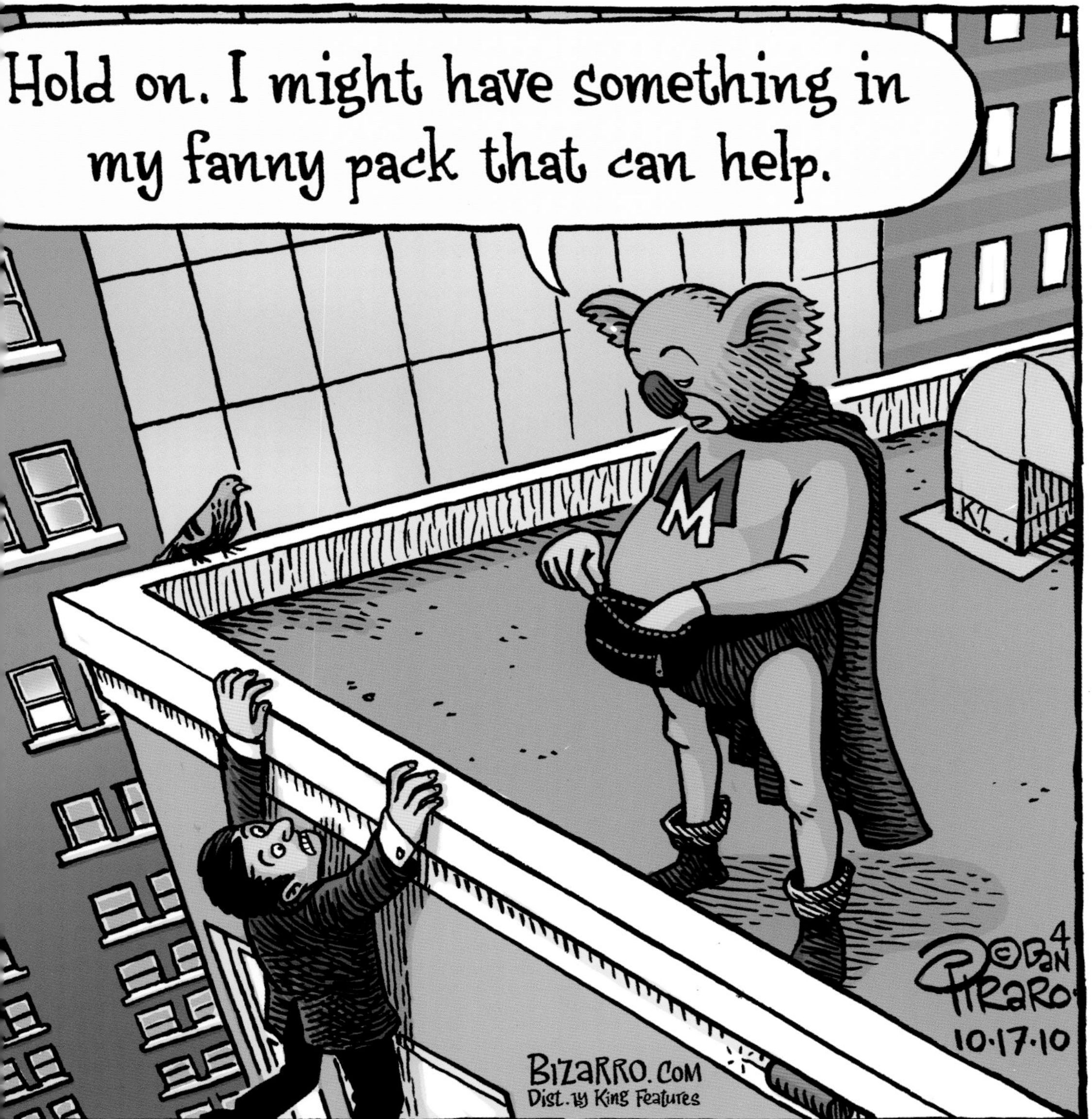
Hold on. I might have something in my fanny pack that can help.
KL
©DAN PIRARO 4
10·17·10
BIZARRO.COM
Dist. by King Features

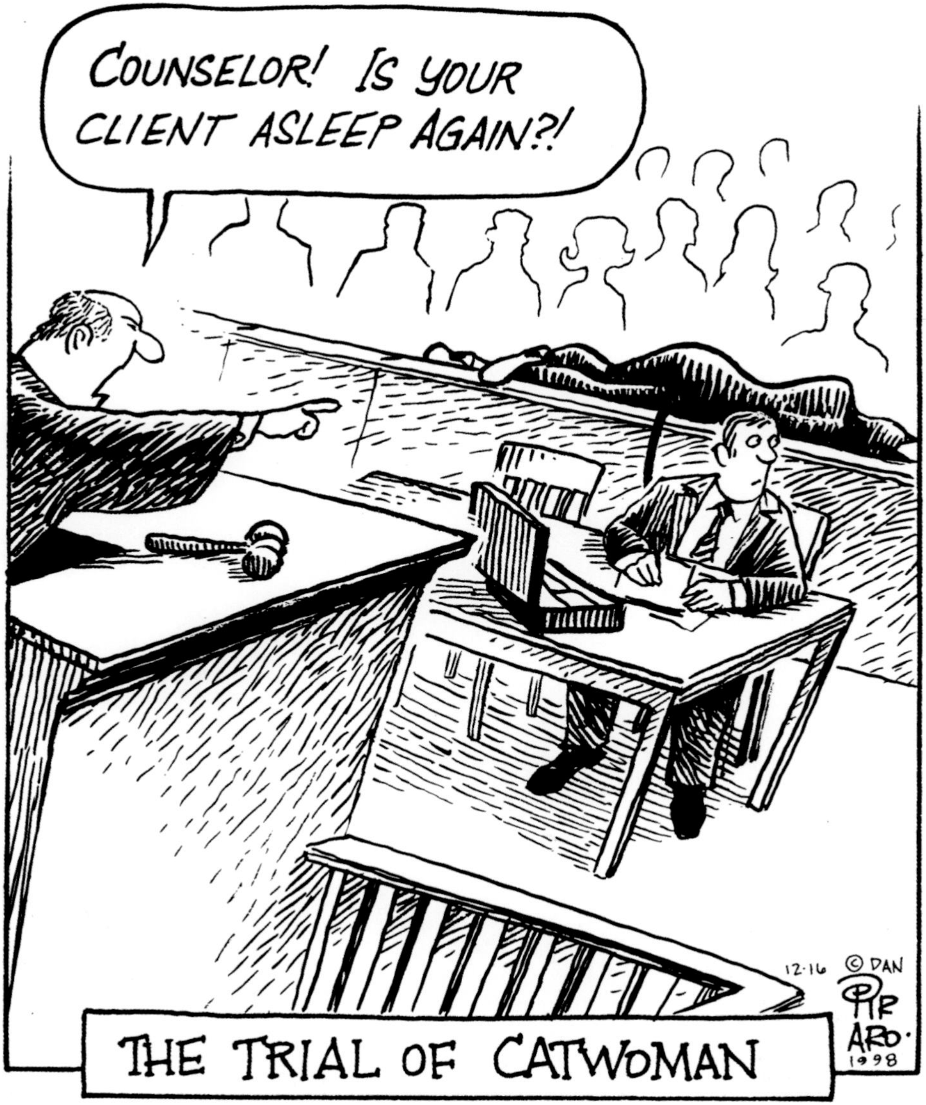
COUNSELOR! IS YOUR CLIENT ASLEEP AGAIN?!
12·16
© DAN PIRARO· 1998

THE TRIAL OF CATWOMAN

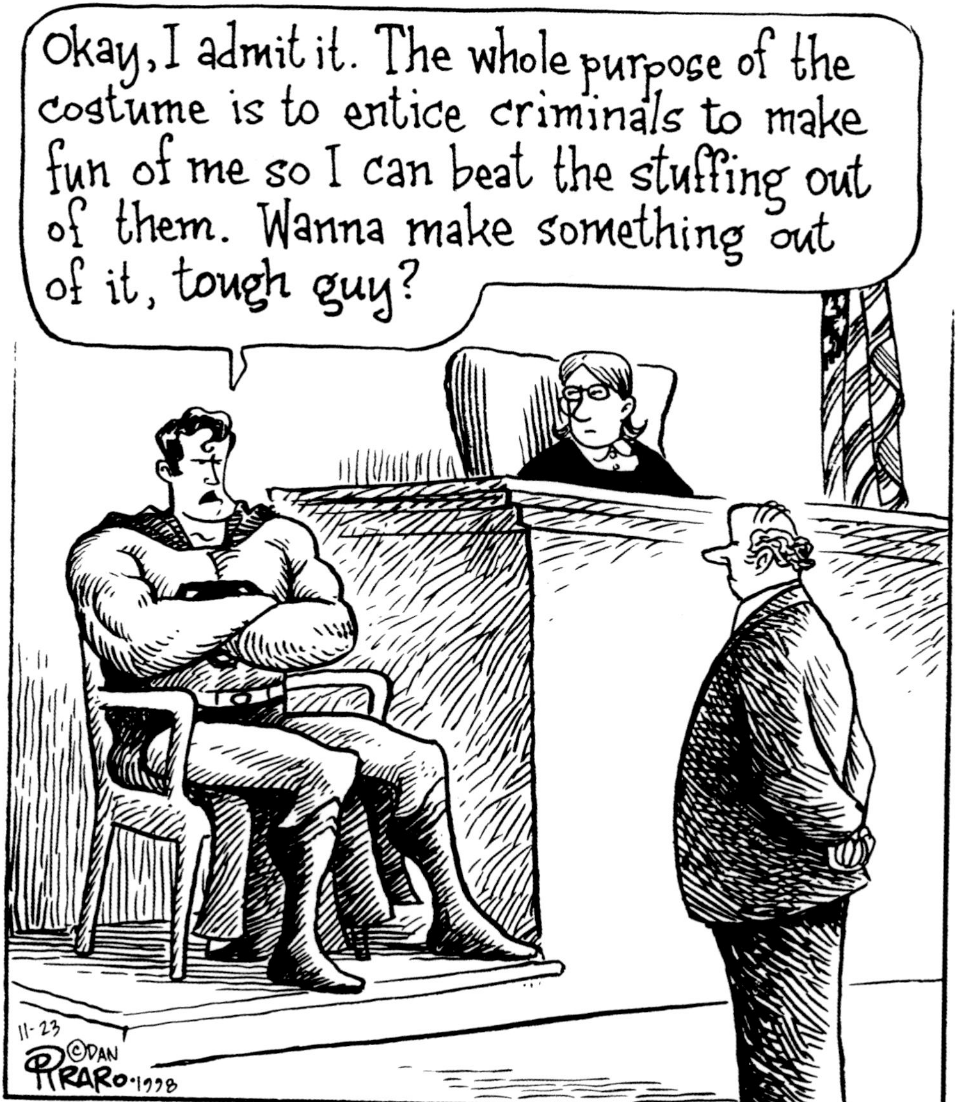
Okay, I admit it. The whole purpose of the costume is to entice criminals to make fun of me so I can beat the stuffing out of them. Wanna make something out of it, tough guy?
11-23
©DAN PIRARO·1998

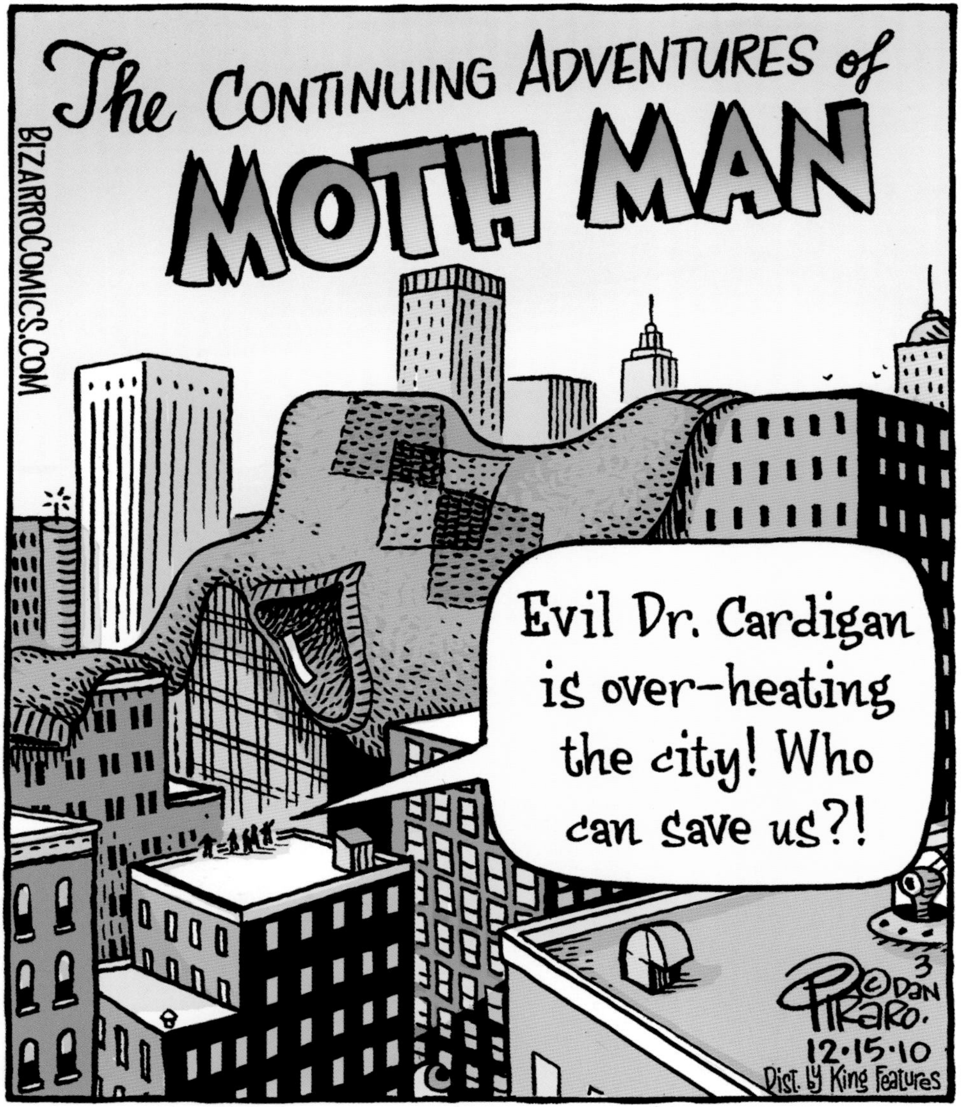
The CONTINUING ADVENTURES of
MOTH MAN
BIZARROCOMICS.COM
Evil Dr. Cardigan is over-heating the city! Who can save us?!
3
© DAN PIRARO.
12·15·10
Dist. by King Features

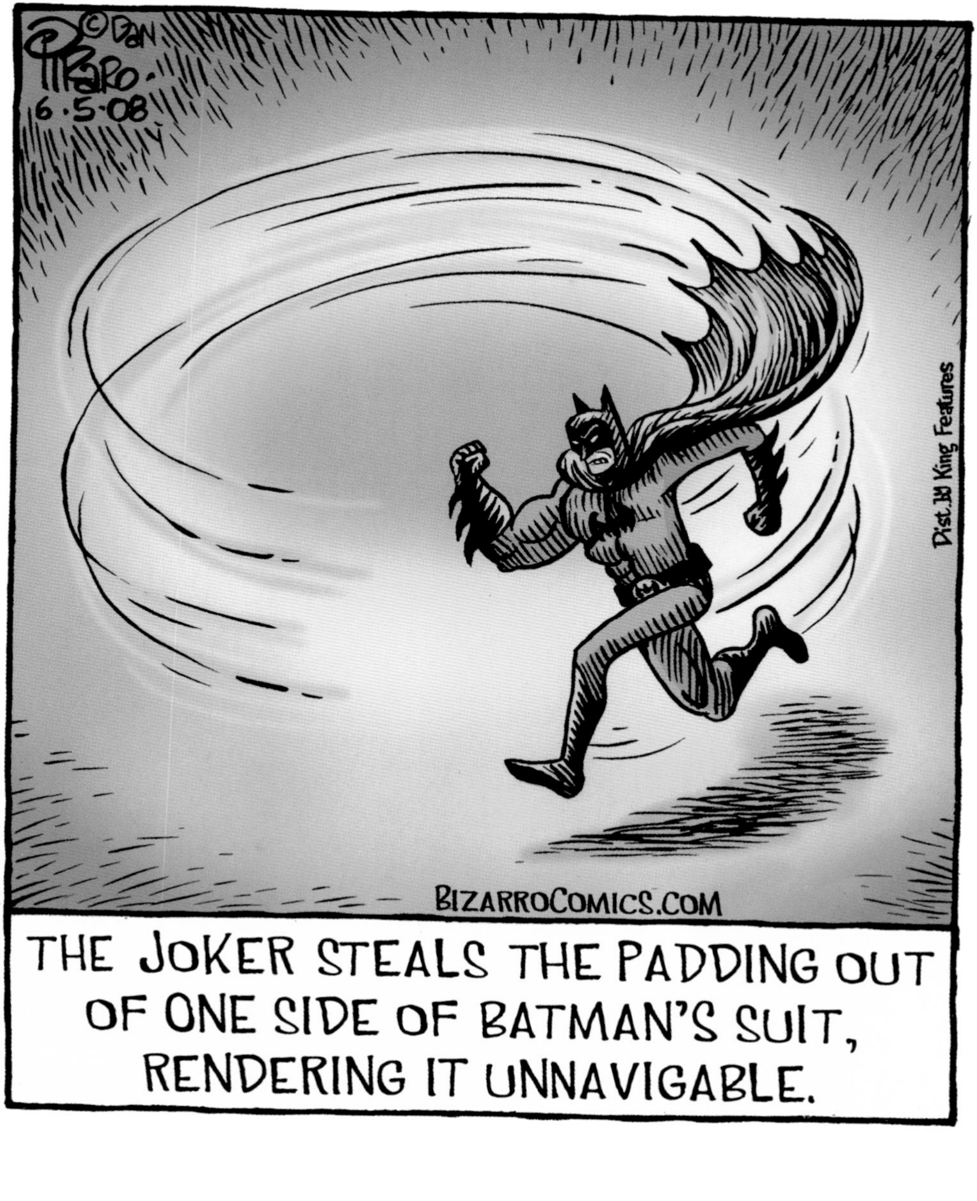
©DAN PIRARO.
6.5.08
Dist. by King Features
BIZARROCOMICS.COM

THE JOKER STEALS THE PADDING OUT OF ONE SIDE OF BATMAN'S SUIT, RENDERING IT UNNAVIGABLE.

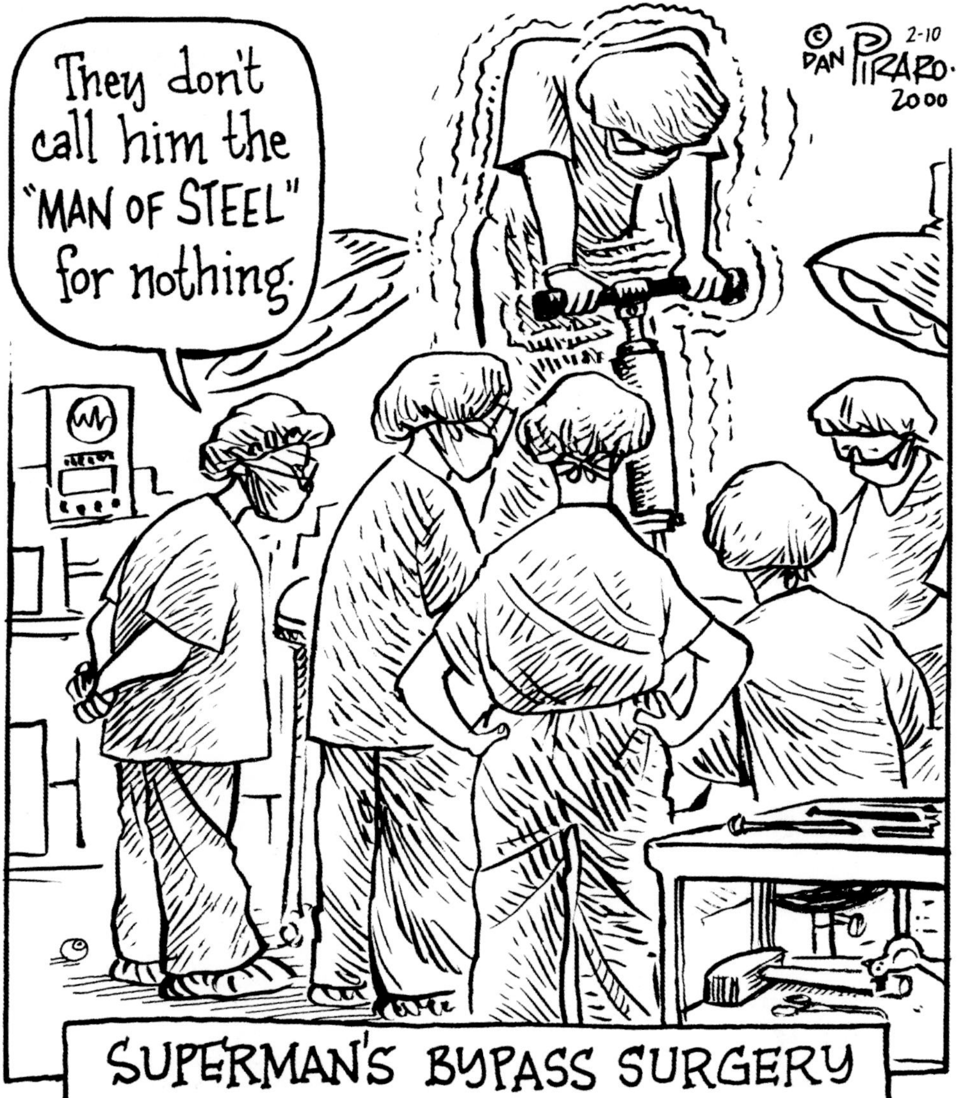
They don't call him the "MAN OF STEEL" for nothing.
© DAN PIRARO 2-10 2000
SUPERMAN'S BYPASS SURGERY

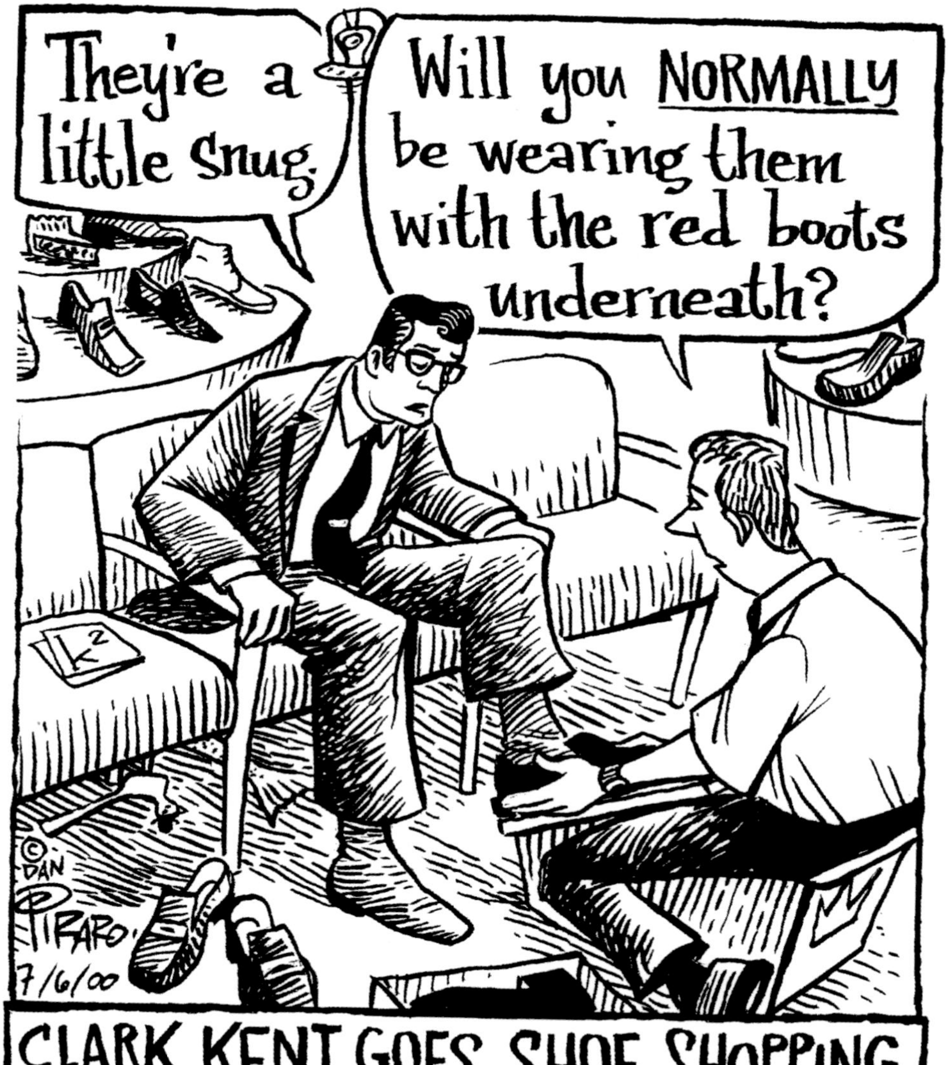
They're a little snug.
Will you NORMALLY be wearing them with the red boots underneath?
© DAN PIRARO 7/6/00
CLARK KENT GOES SHOE SHOPPING

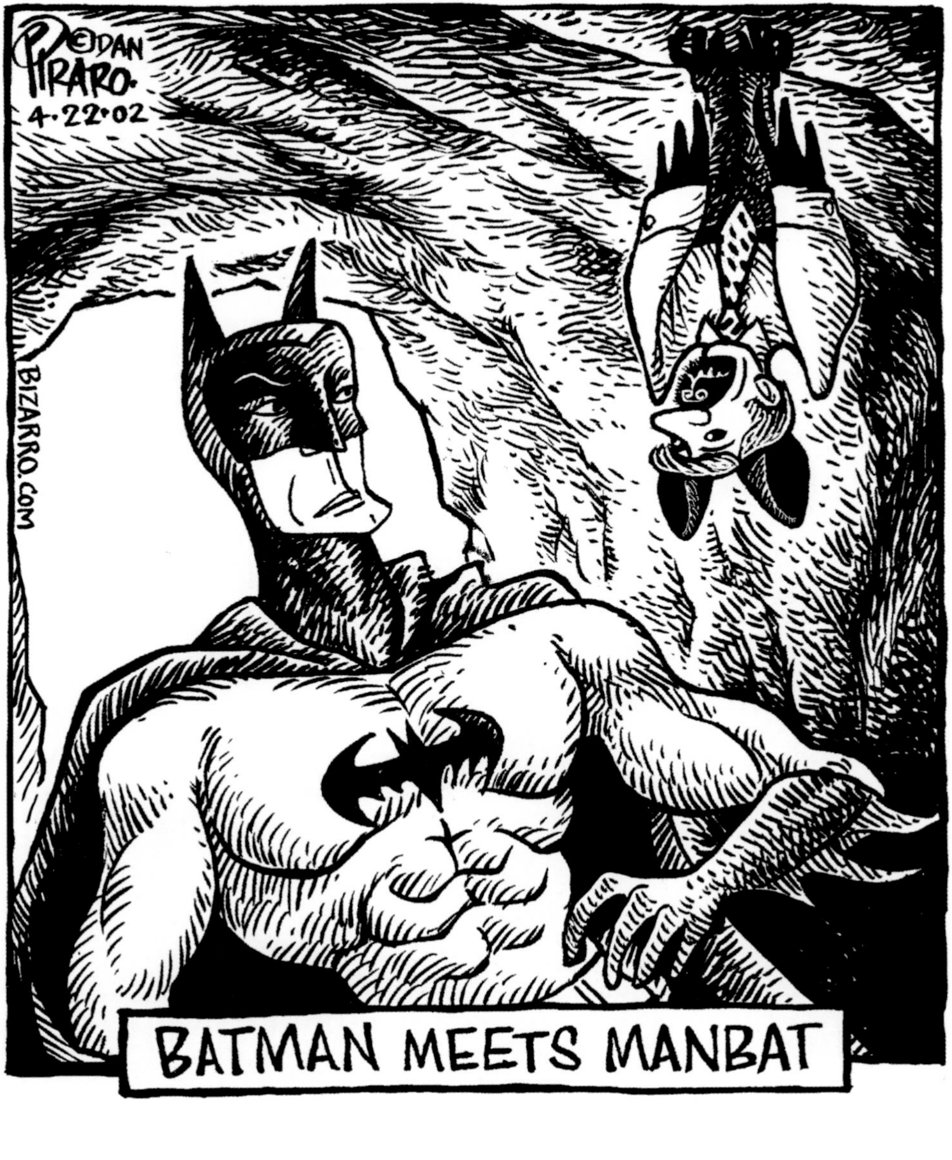
©DAN PIRARO 4·22·02
BIZARRO.COM
BATMAN MEETS MANBAT

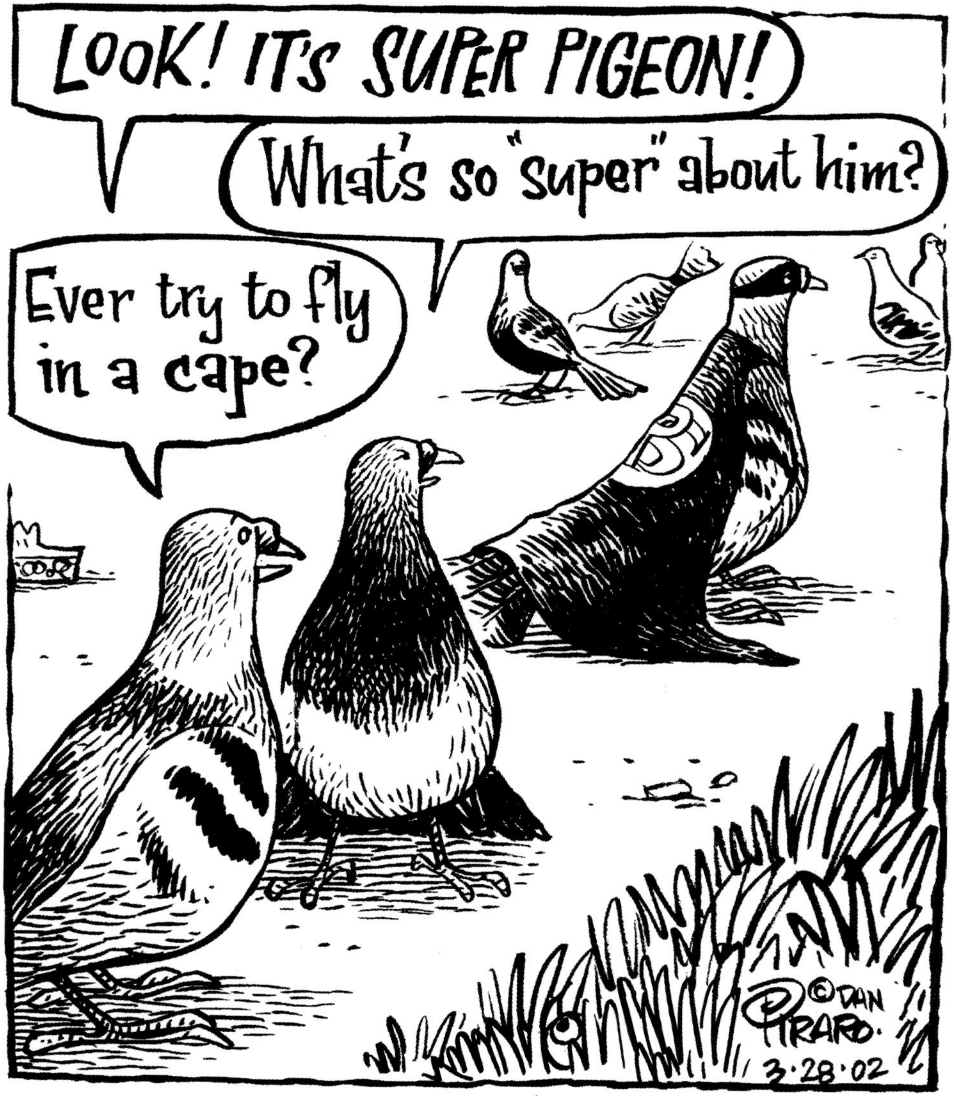
LOOK! IT'S SUPER PIGEON!
What's so "super" about him?
Ever try to fly in a cape?
©DAN PIRARO 3·28·02

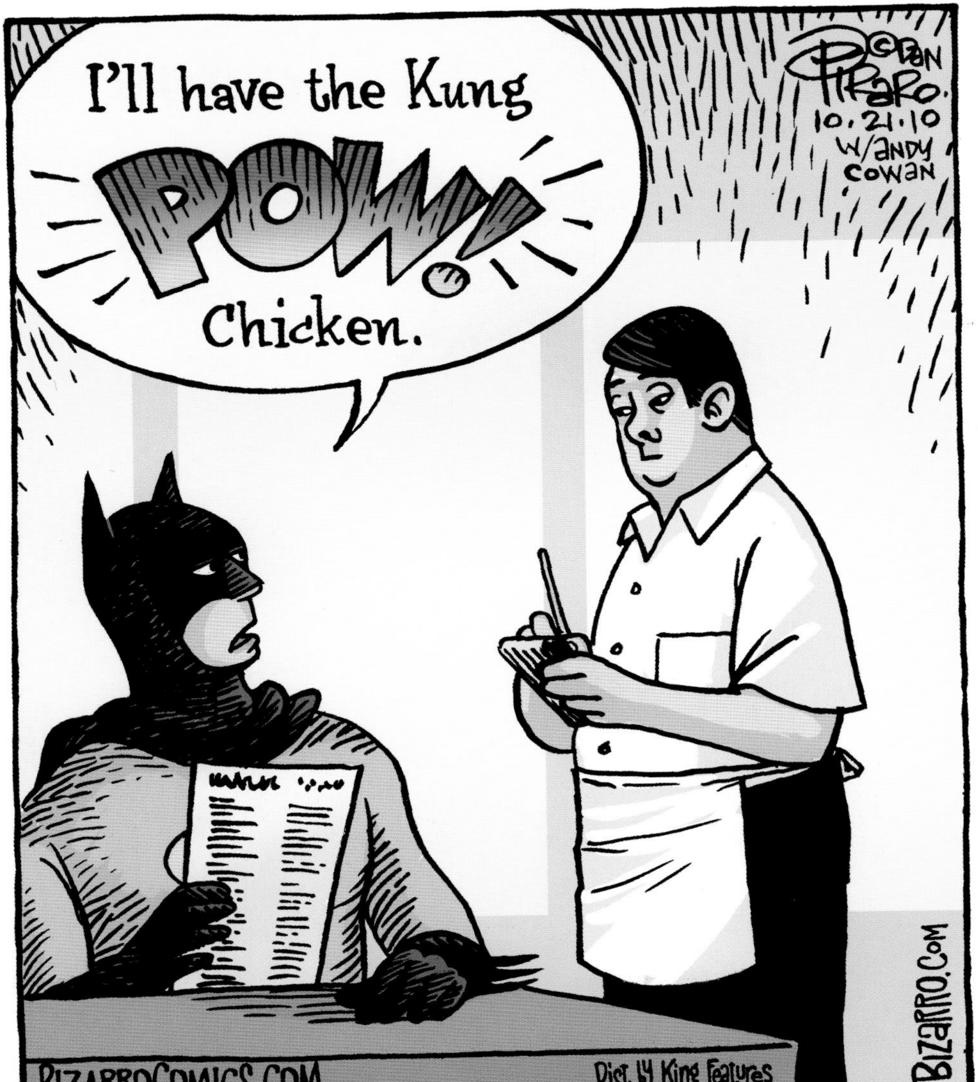
I'll have the Kung
POW!
Chicken.
©DAN PIRARO 10.21.10 w/ANDY COWAN
BIZARROCOMICS.COM
Dist. by King Features
BIZARRO.COM

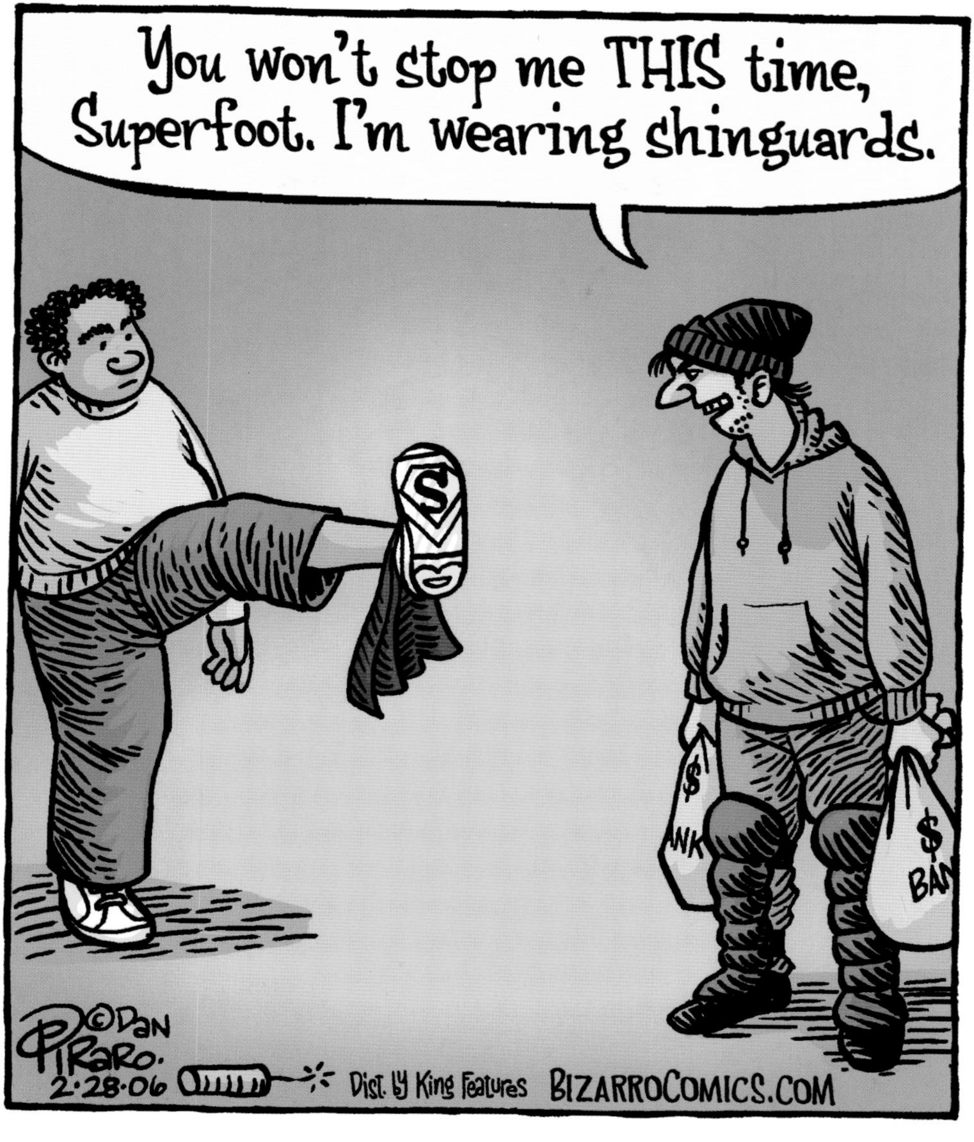
You won't stop me THIS time, Superfoot. I'm wearing shinguards.
S
$
NK
$
BAN
©DAN PIRARO. 2·28·06
Dist. by King Features
BIZARROCOMICS.COM

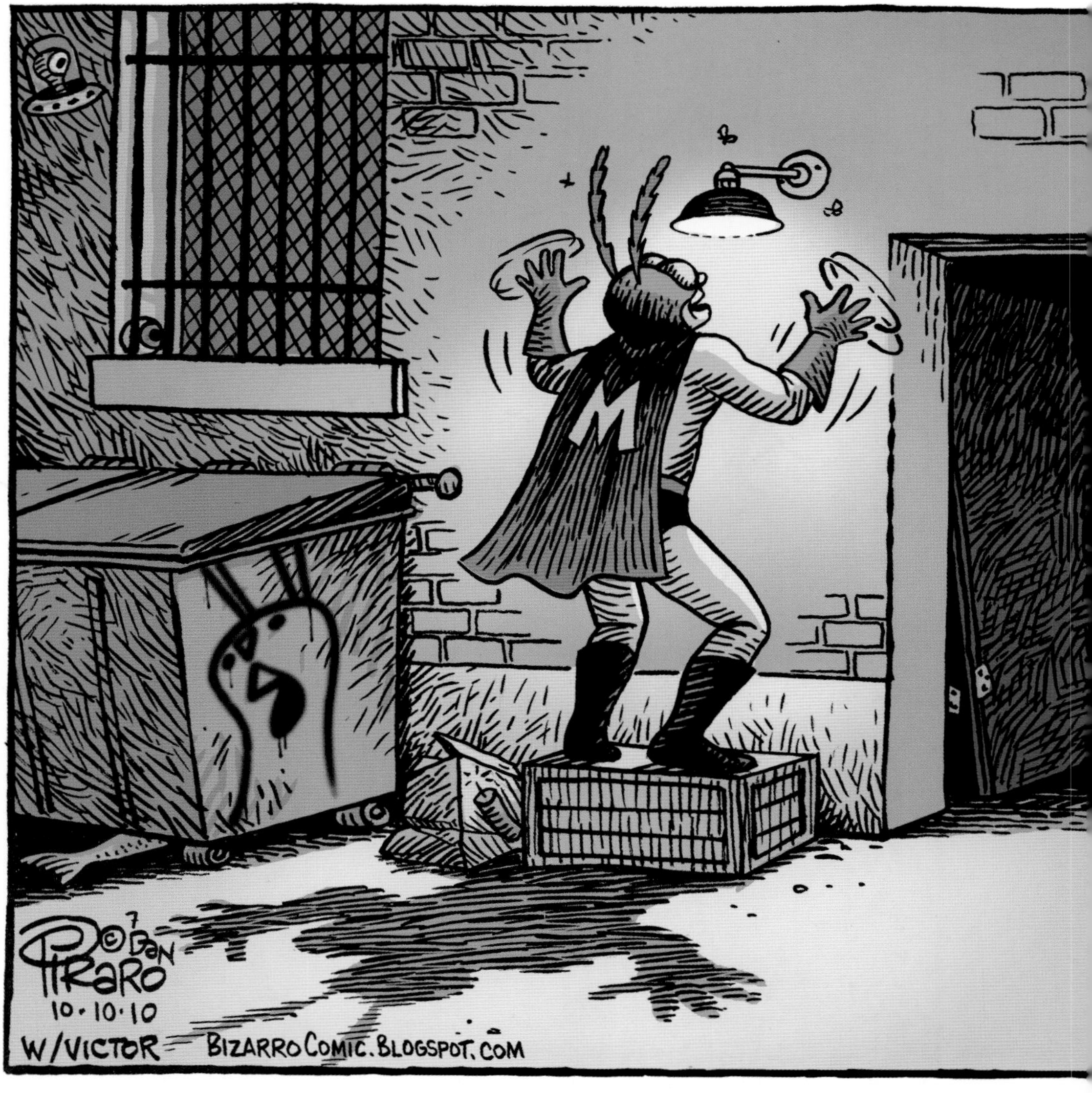
©DAN PIRARO 10·10·10
W/VICTOR
BIZARROCOMIC.BLOGSPOT.COM

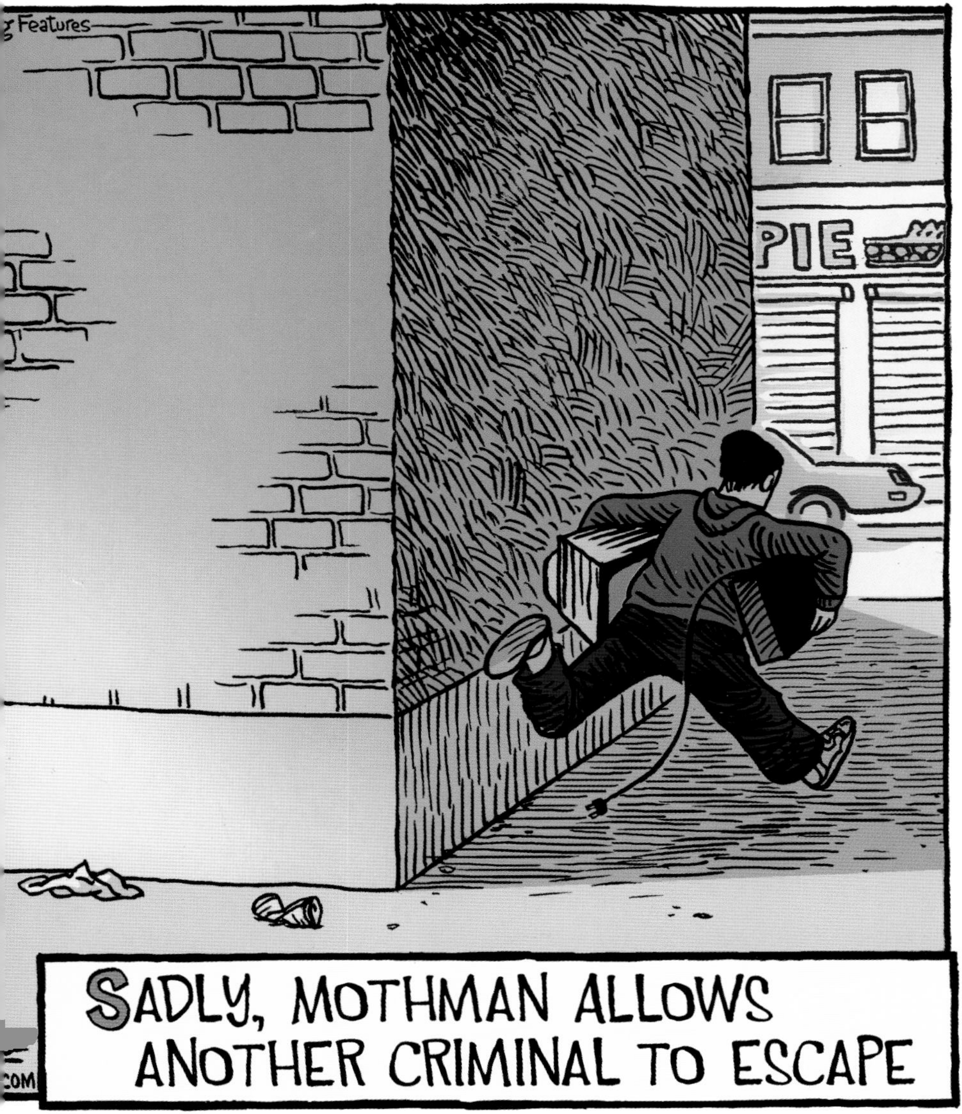
PIE
SADLY, MOTHMAN ALLOWS ANOTHER CRIMINAL TO ESCAPE

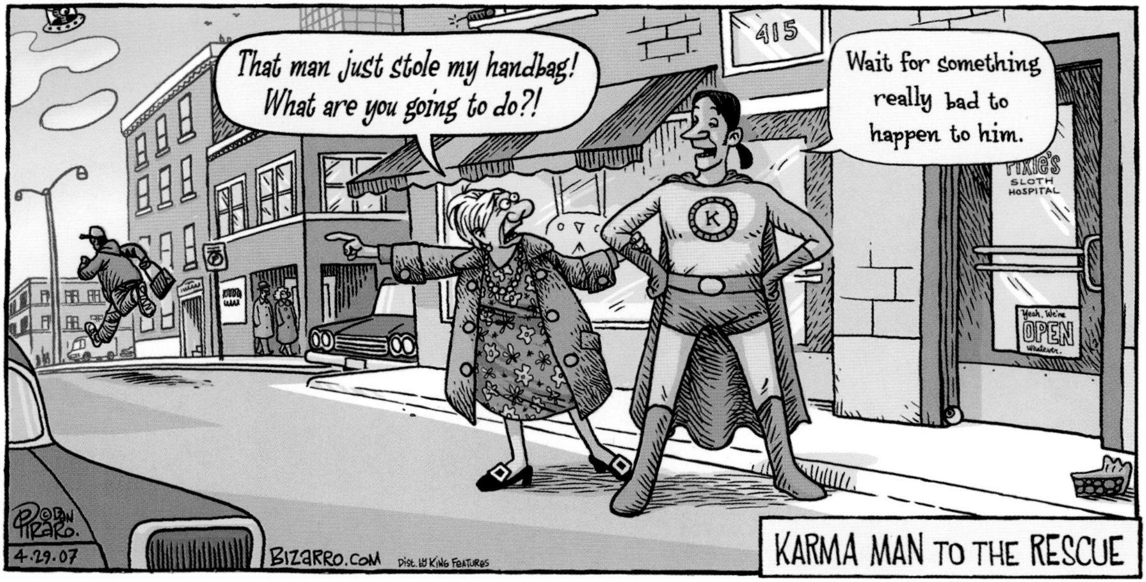
That man just stole my handbag! What are you going to do?!
Wait for something really bad to happen to him.
415
Pixie's SLOTH HOSPITAL
Yeah, We're OPEN whatever.
©DAN PIRARO.
4-29-07
BIZARRO.COM
Dist. by King Features
KARMA MAN TO THE RESCUE

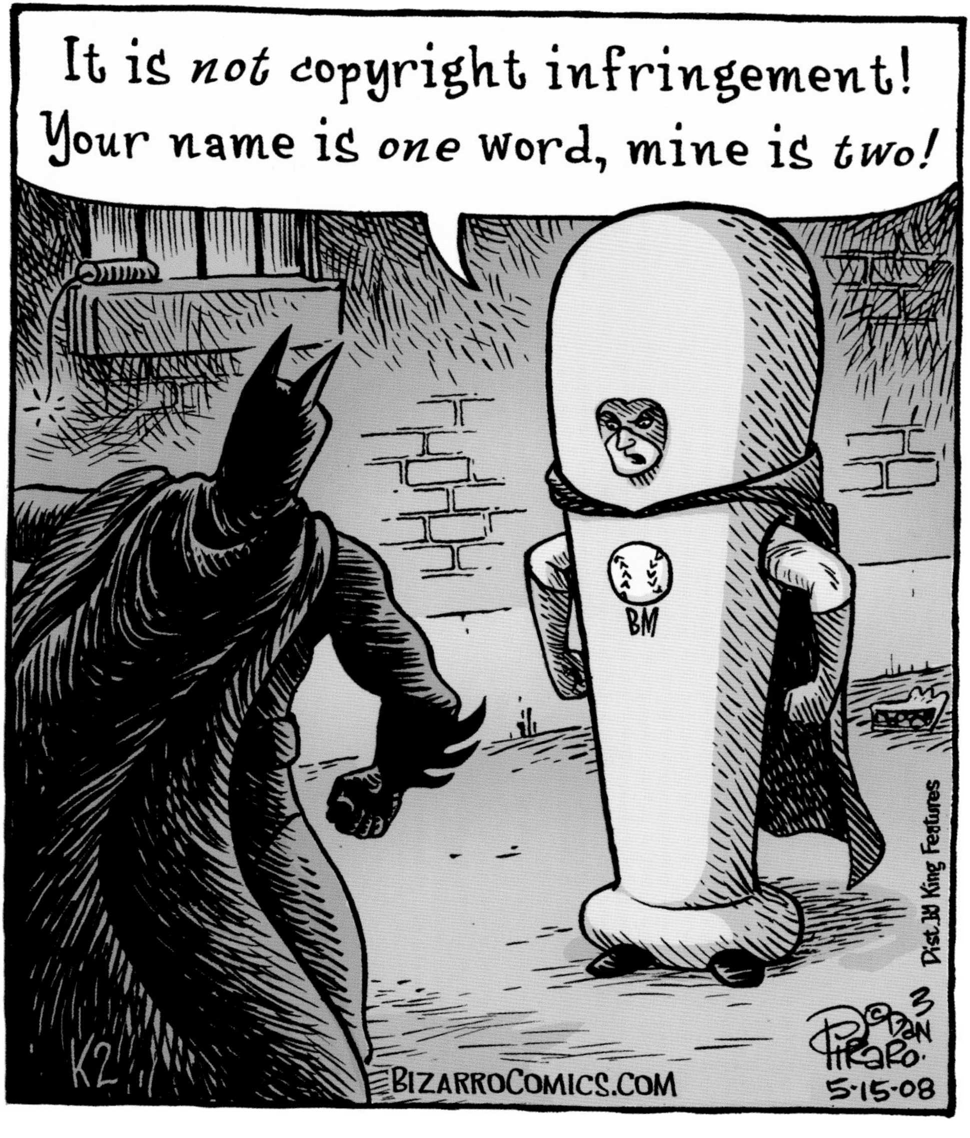
It is *not* copyright infringement! Your name is *one* word, mine is *two*!
BM
Dist. by King Features
© Dan Piraro 5-15-08
K2
BIZARROCOMICS.COM

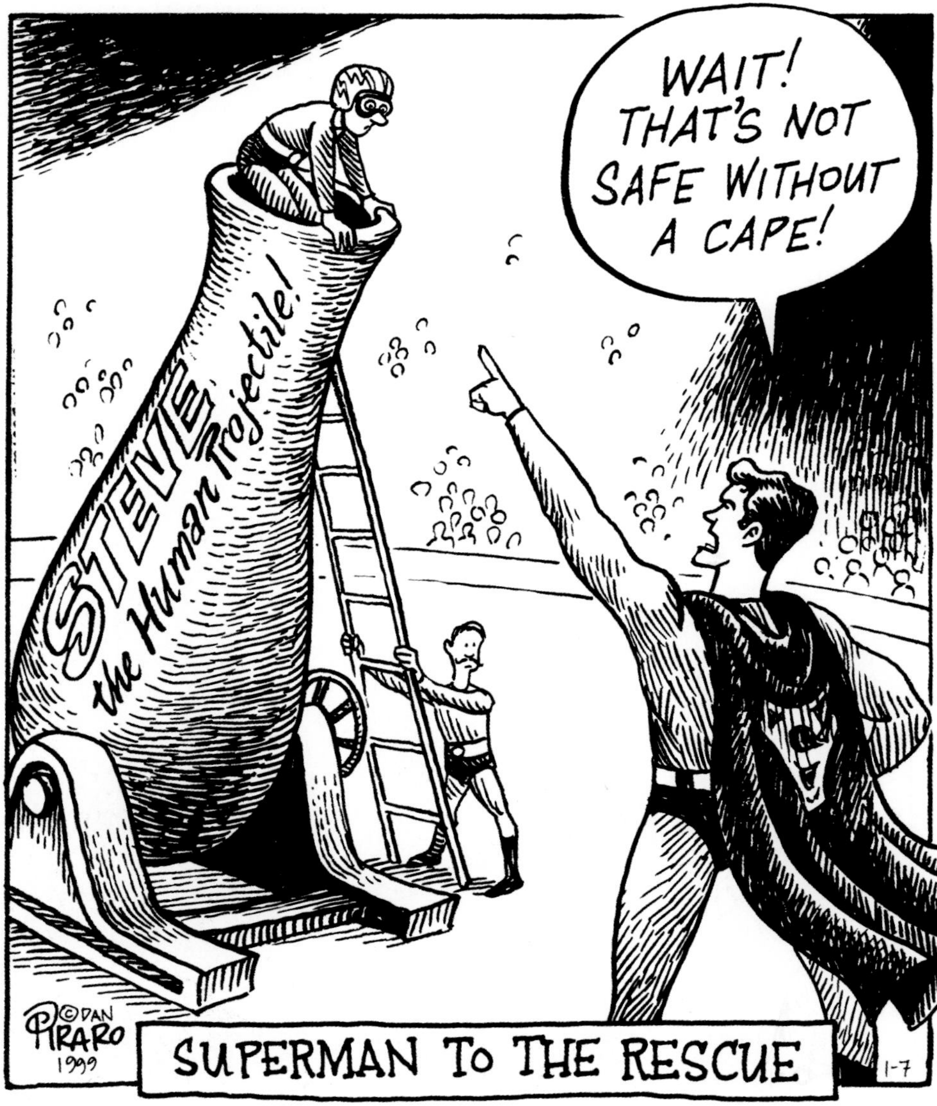
STEVE the Human Projectile!
WAIT! THAT'S NOT SAFE WITHOUT A CAPE!
©DAN PIRARO 1999
SUPERMAN TO THE RESCUE
1-7

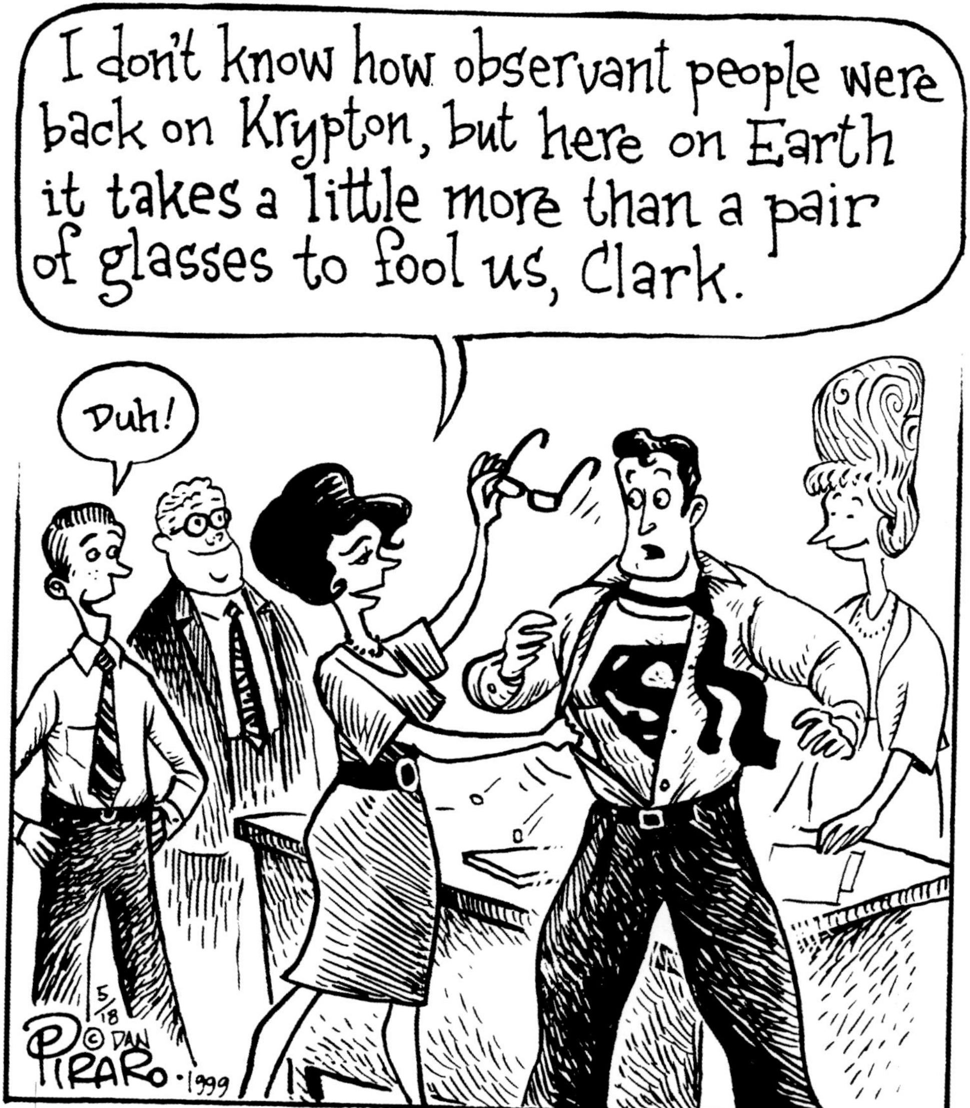
I don't know how observant people were back on Krypton, but here on Earth it takes a little more than a pair of glasses to fool us, Clark.
Duh!
5/18 © DAN PIRARO · 1999

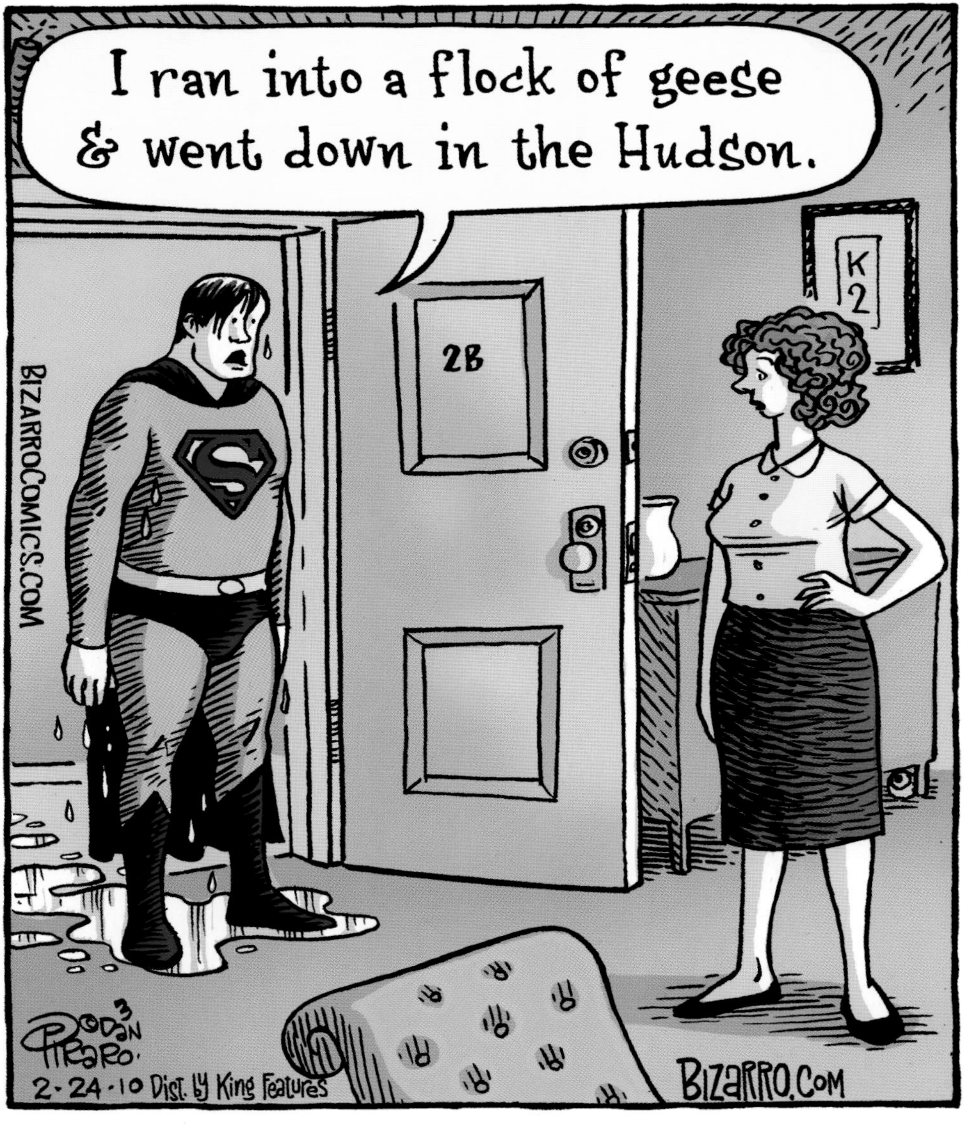
I ran into a flock of geese & went down in the Hudson.
2B
K2
BIZARROCOMICS.COM
DAN PIRARO
2-24-10 Dist. by King Features
BIZARRO.COM

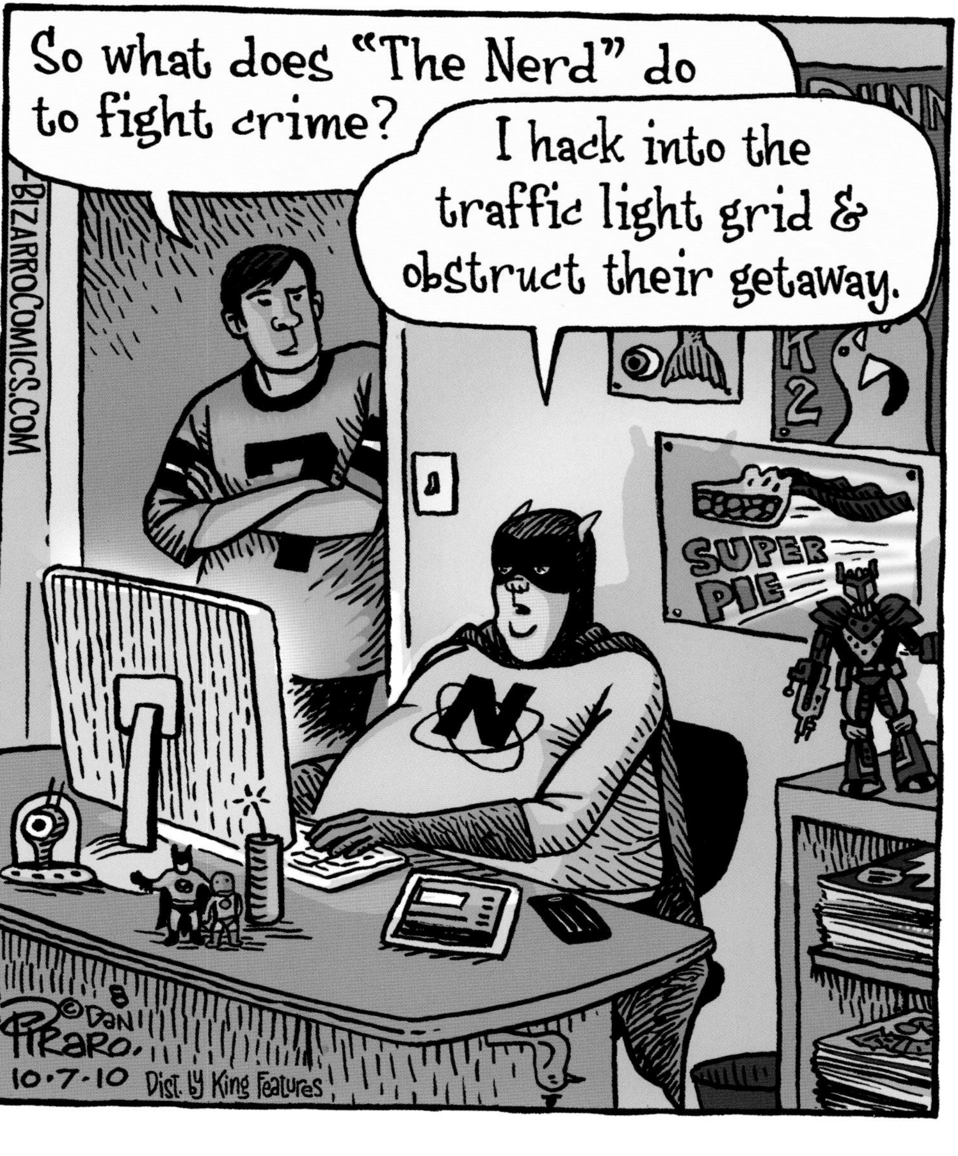
So what does "The Nerd" do to fight crime?
I hack into the traffic light grid & obstruct their getaway.
BIZARROCOMICS.COM
SUPER PIE
© Dan Piraro. 10-7-10 Dist. by King Features

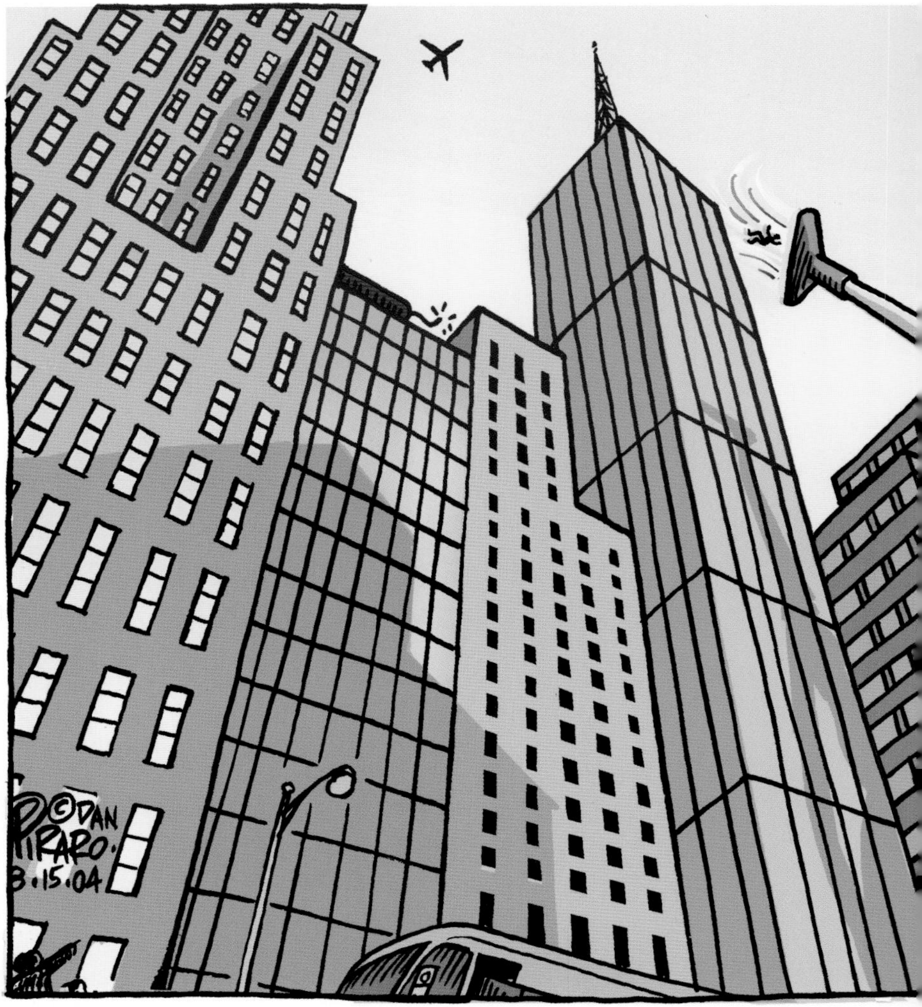
©DAN PIRARO. 8.15.04

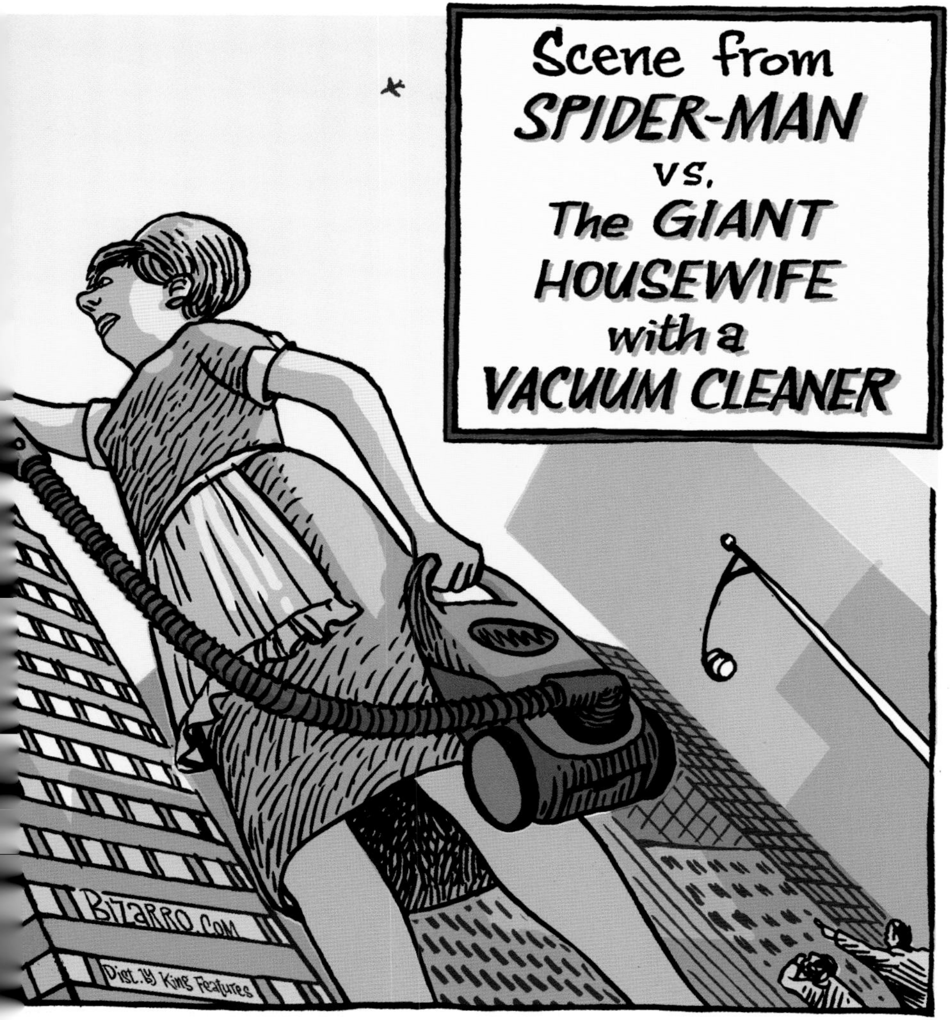
Scene from
SPIDER-MAN
vs.
The GIANT
HOUSEWIFE
with a
VACUUM CLEANER
BIZARRO.COM
Dist. by King Features

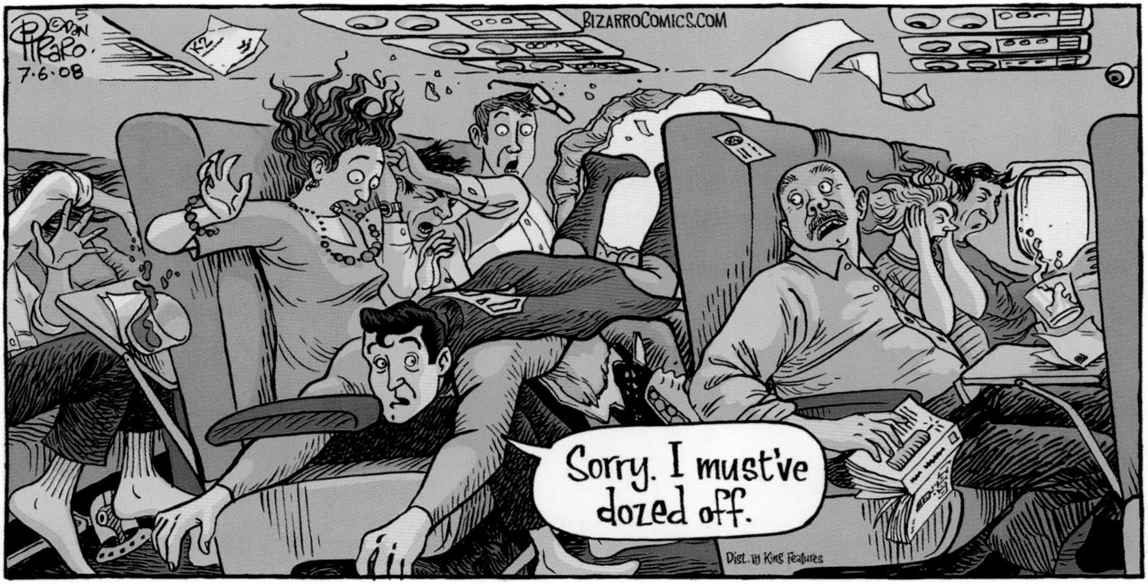
©DAN PIRARO 7·6·08
BIZARROCOMICS.COM
Sorry. I must've dozed off.
Dist. by King Features

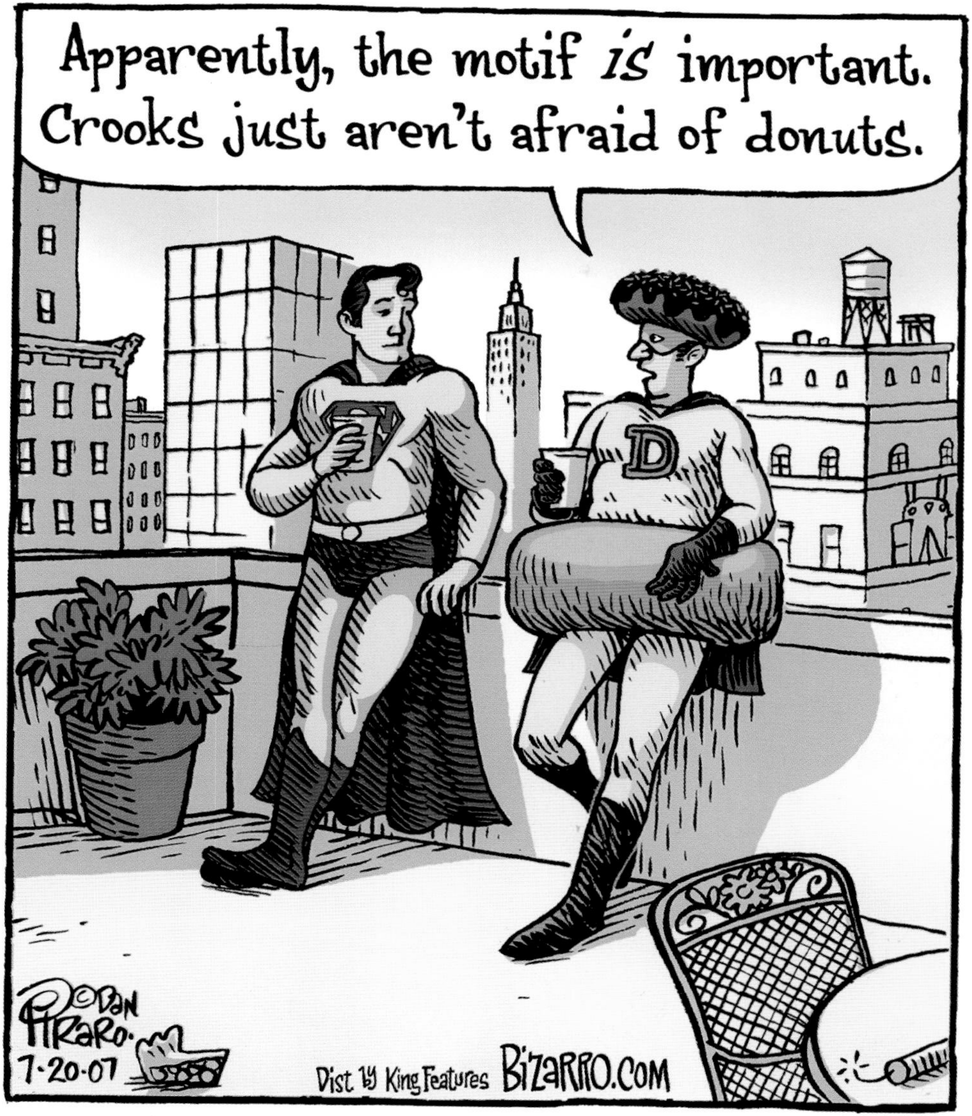
Apparently, the motif *is* important. Crooks just aren't afraid of donuts.
D
©Dan Piraro
7-20-07
Dist. by King Features
Bizarro.com

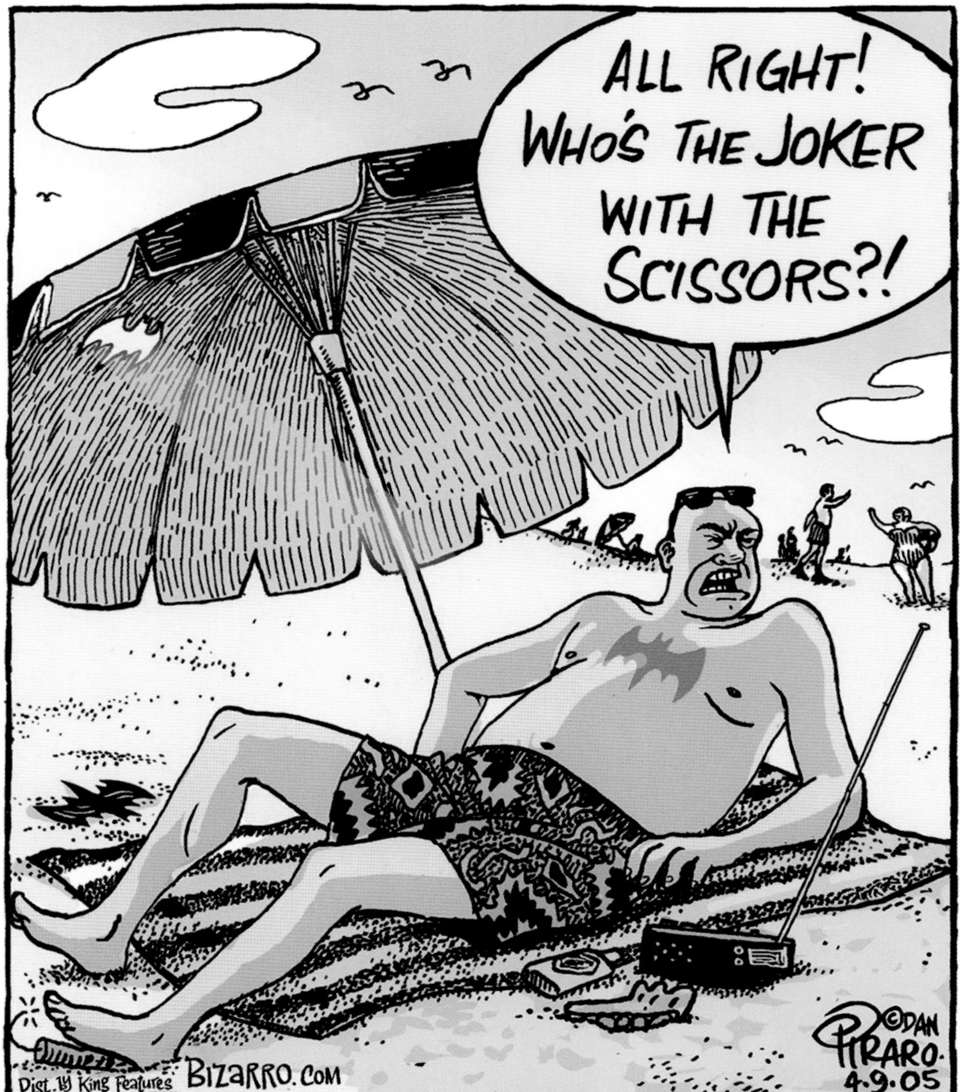
ALL RIGHT! WHO'S THE JOKER WITH THE SCISSORS?!
Dist. by King Features BIZARRO.COM
©DAN PIRARO 4.9.05

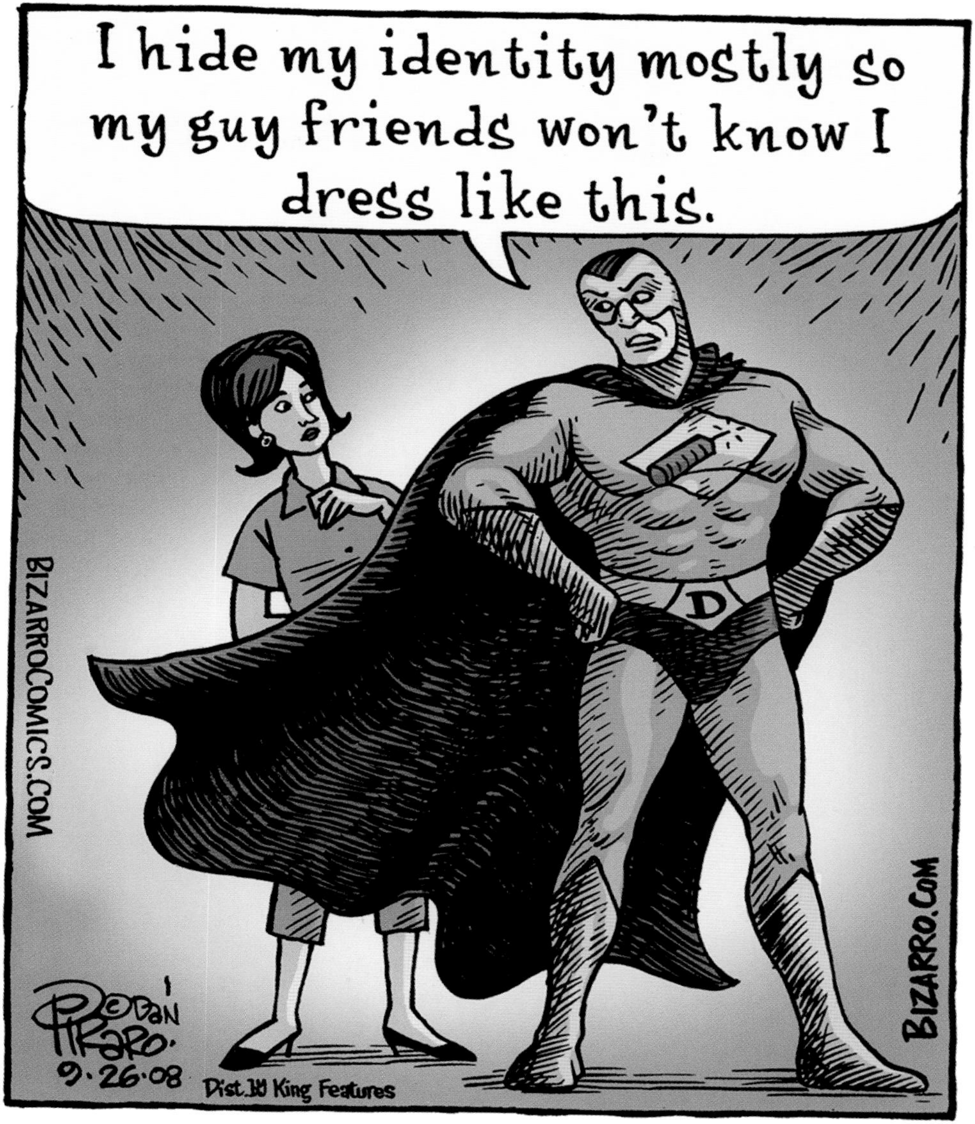
I hide my identity mostly so my guy friends won't know I dress like this.
D
D
BIZARROCOMICS.COM
BIZARRO.COM
DAN PIRARO
9.26.08
Dist. by King Features

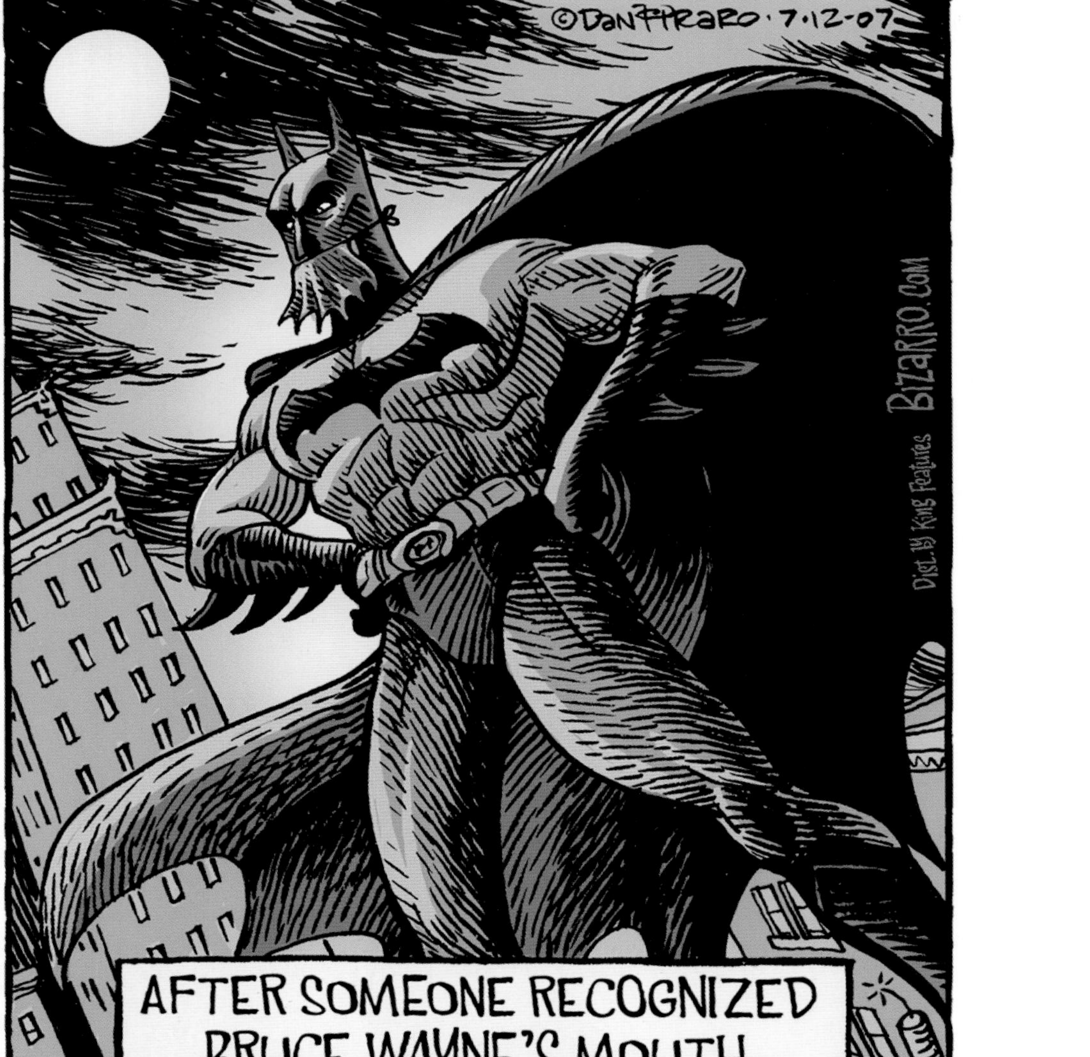
©DAN PIRARO·7·12·07
BIZARRO.COM
Dist. by King Features
AFTER SOMEONE RECOGNIZED
BRUCE WAYNE'S MOUTH

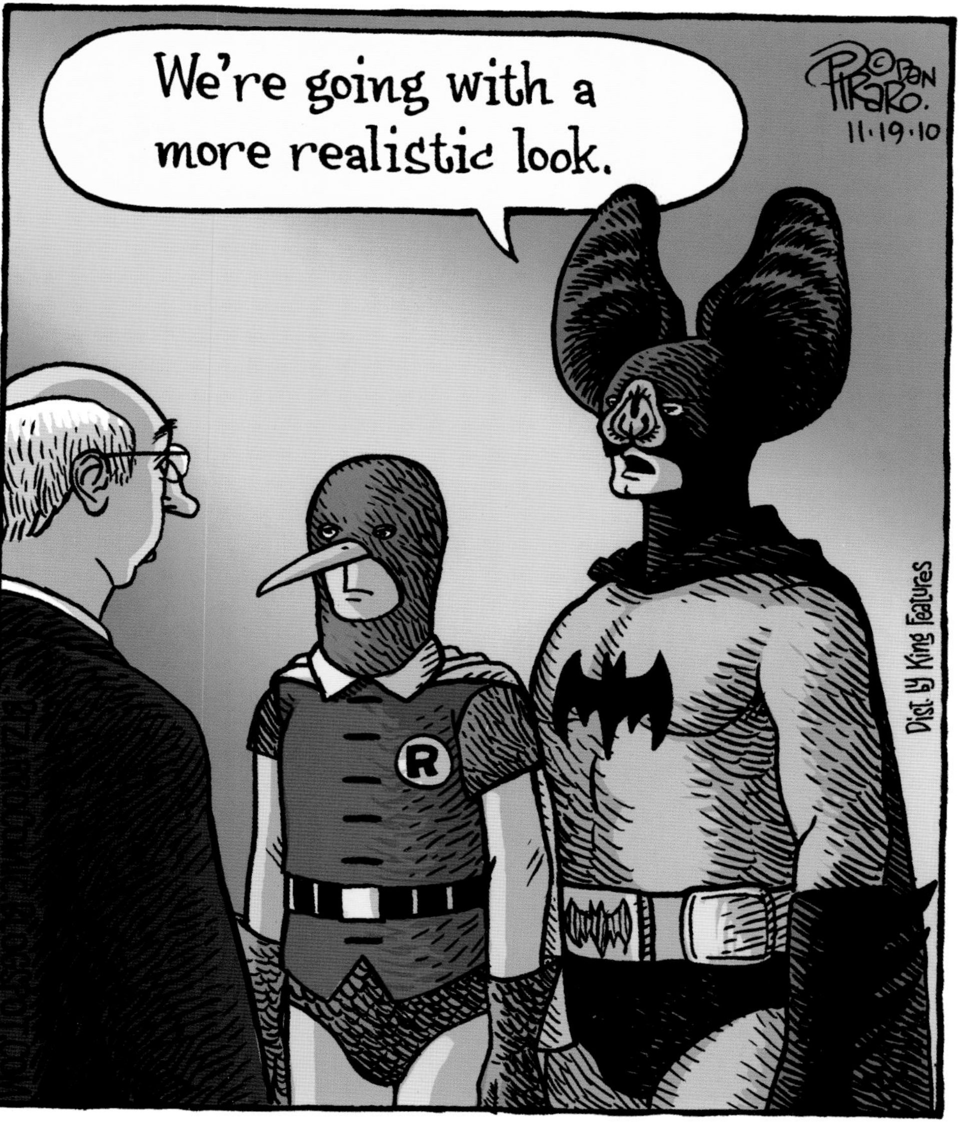
We're going with a more realistic look.
©Dan Piraro. 11·19·10
Dist. by King Features

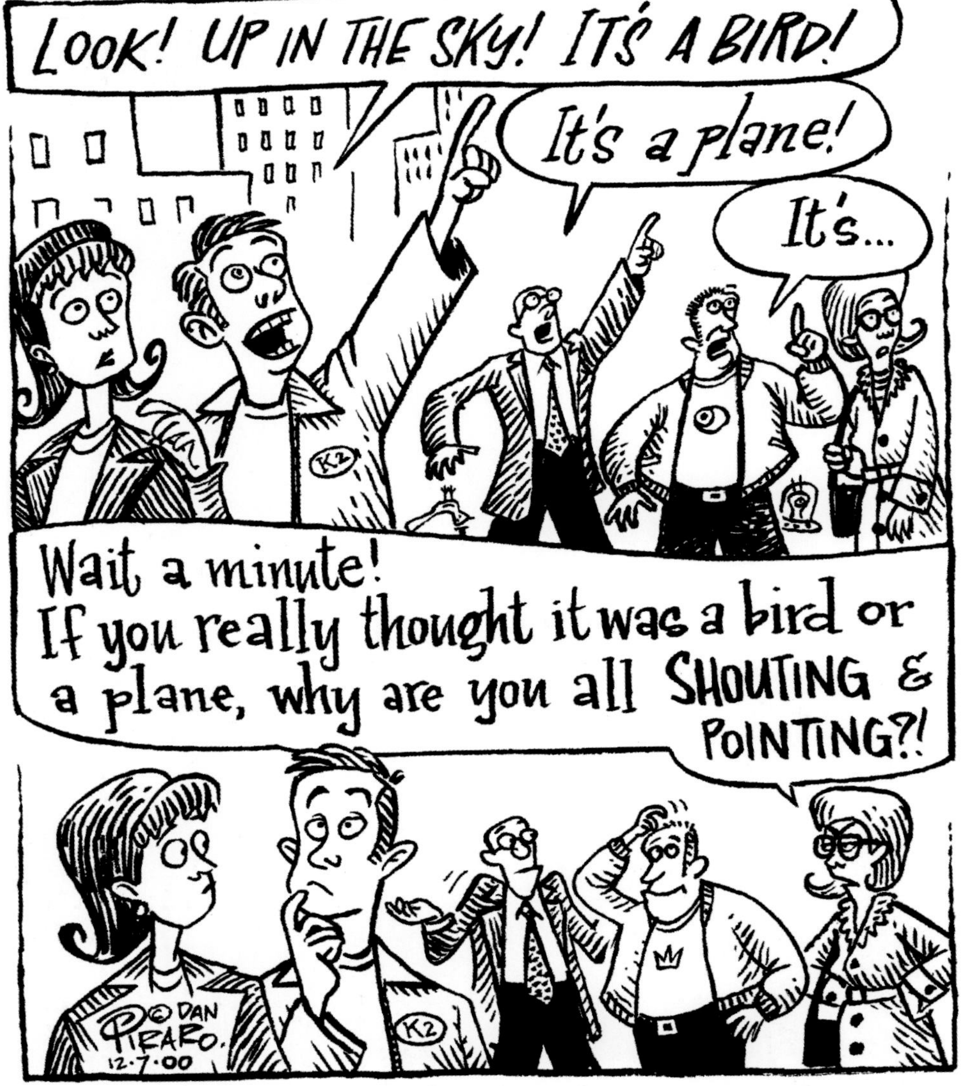
LOOK! UP IN THE SKY! IT'S A BIRD!
It's a plane!
It's...
Wait a minute!
If you really thought it was a bird or a plane, why are you all SHOUTING & POINTING?!
© DAN PIRARO. 12·7·00

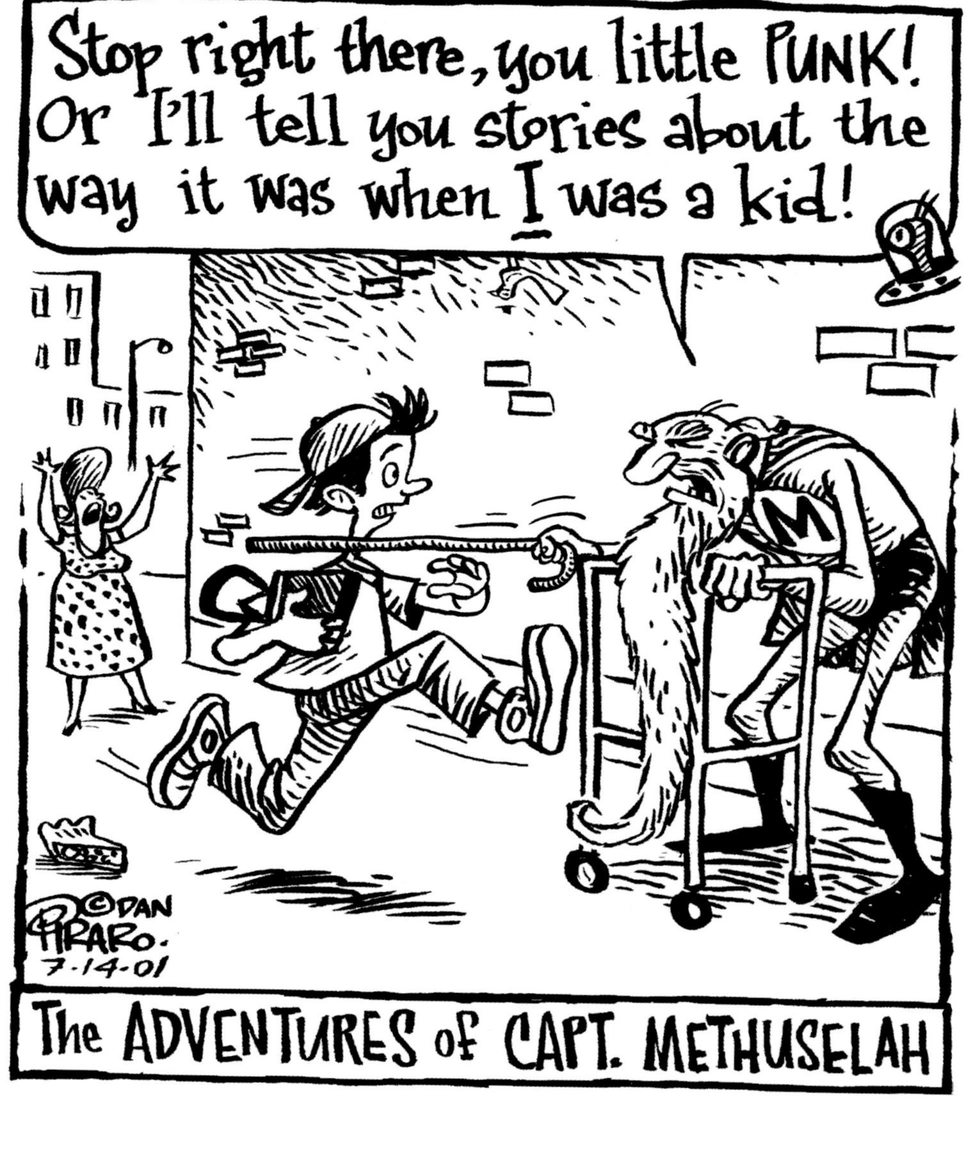
Stop right there, you little PUNK! Or I'll tell you stories about the way it was when I was a kid!
©DAN PIRARO. 7-14-01

The ADVENTURES of CAPT. METHUSELAH

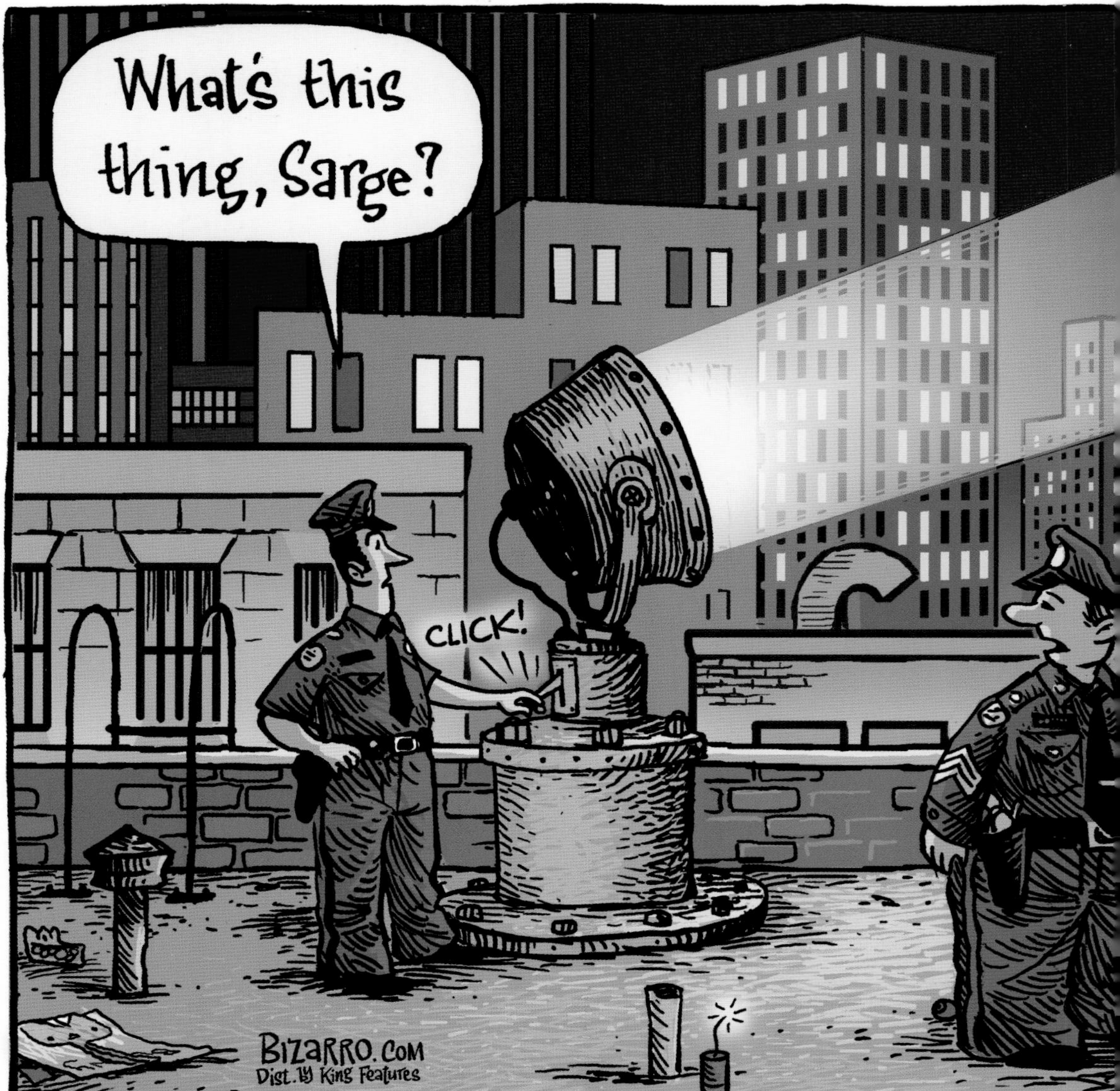
What's this thing, Sarge?
CLICK!
BIZARRO.COM
Dist. by King Features

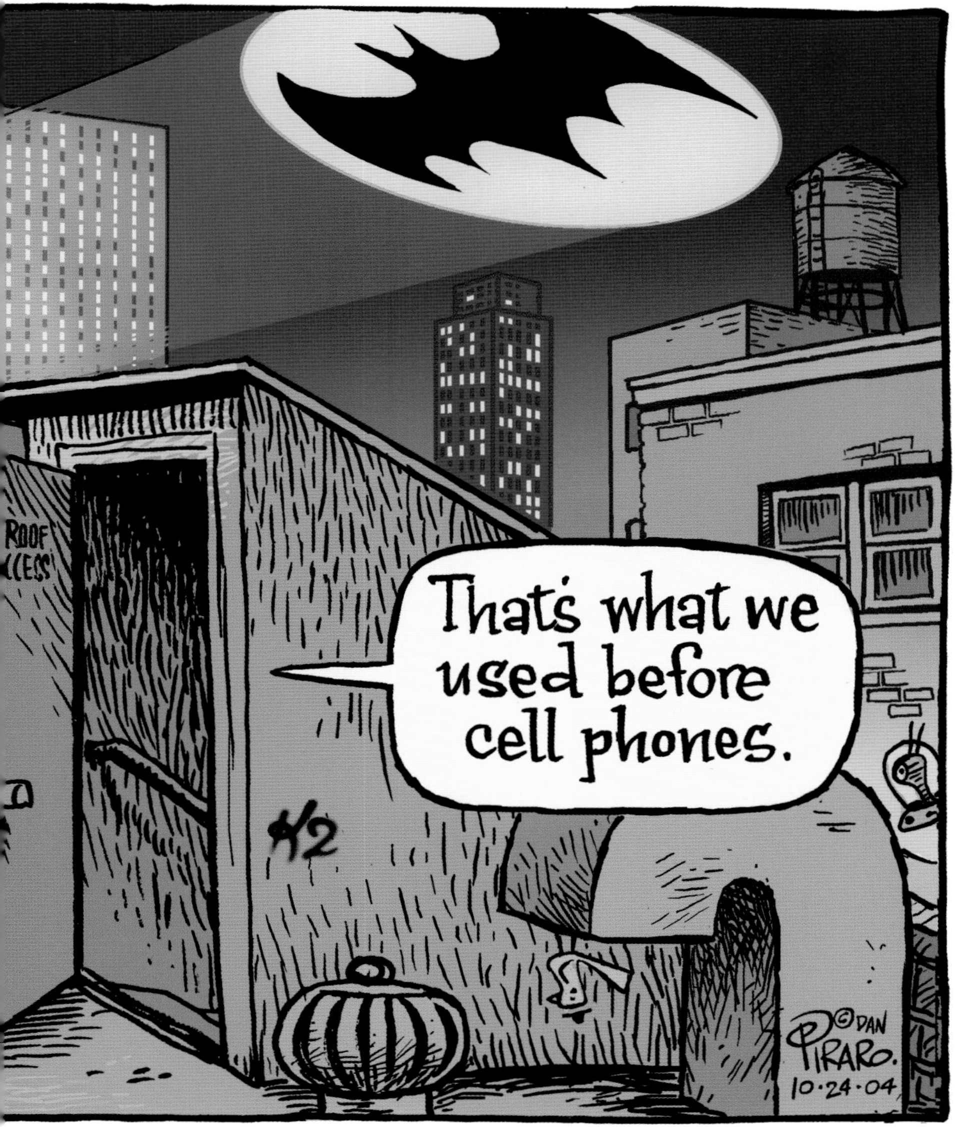
That's what we used before cell phones.
ROOF
CCESS
©DAN PIRARO.
10·24·04

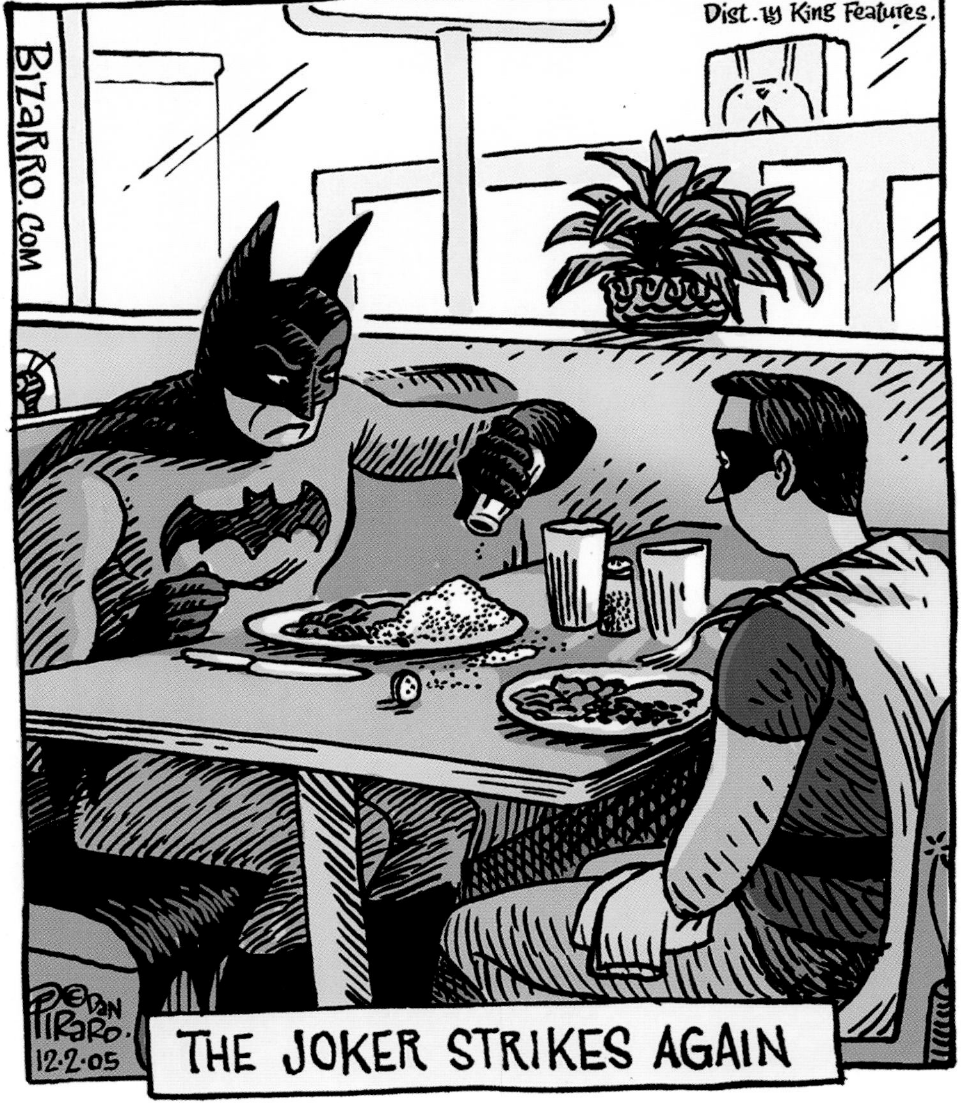
Dist. by King Features.
BIZARRO.COM
©DAN PIRARO.
12·2·05
THE JOKER STRIKES AGAIN

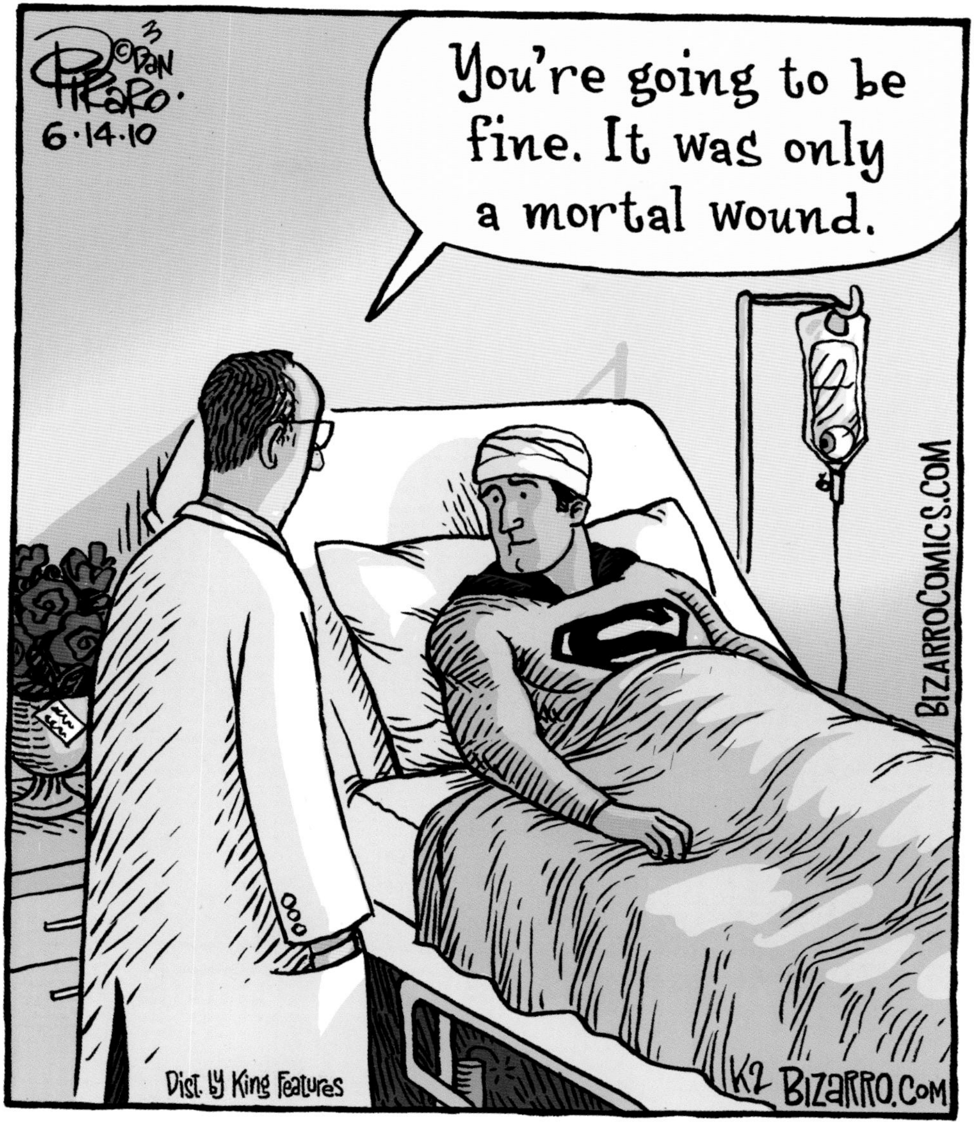
©Dan Piraro 6·14·10
You're going to be fine. It was only a mortal wound.
BIZARROCOMICS.COM
Dist. by King Features
K2 BIZARRO.COM

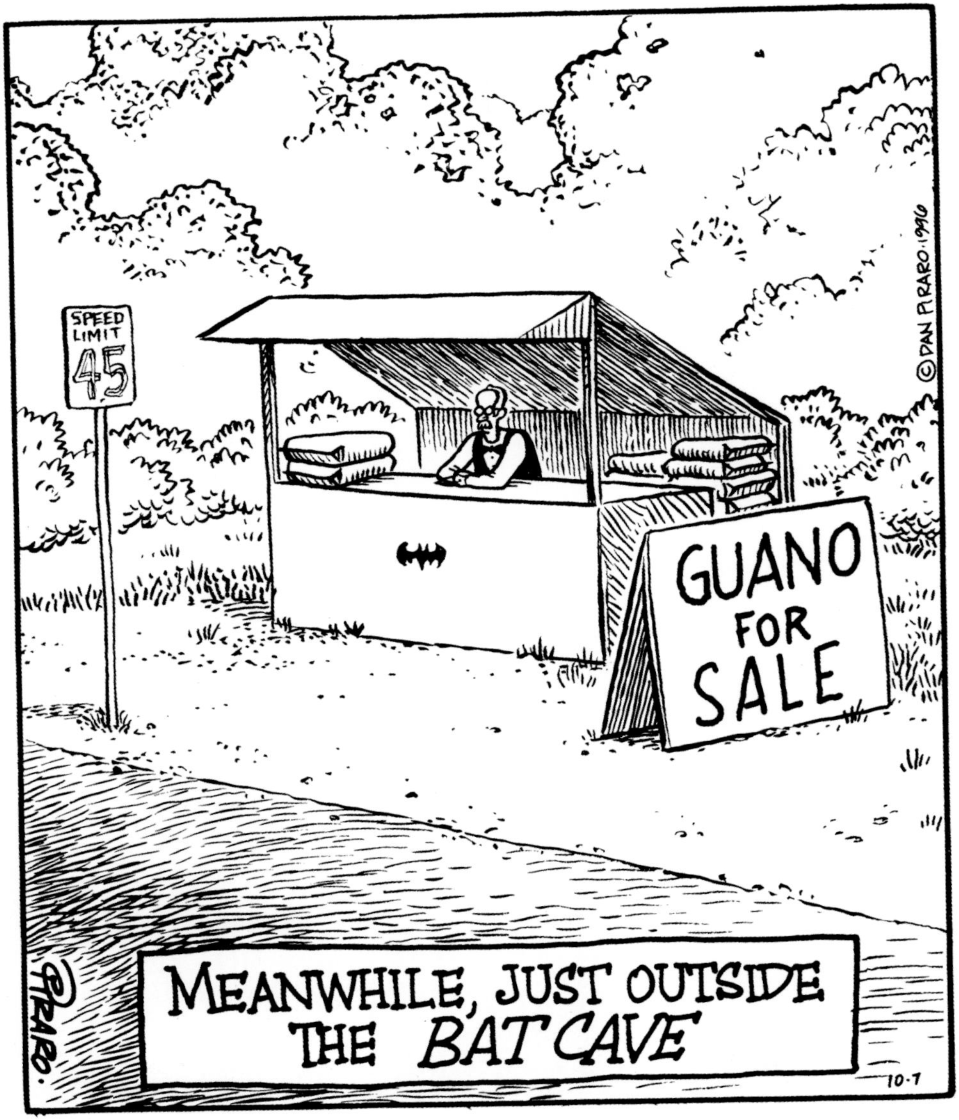
SPEED LIMIT 45
GUANO FOR SALE
©DAN PIRARO·1996
MEANWHILE, JUST OUTSIDE THE *BAT CAVE*
PIRARO.
10-7

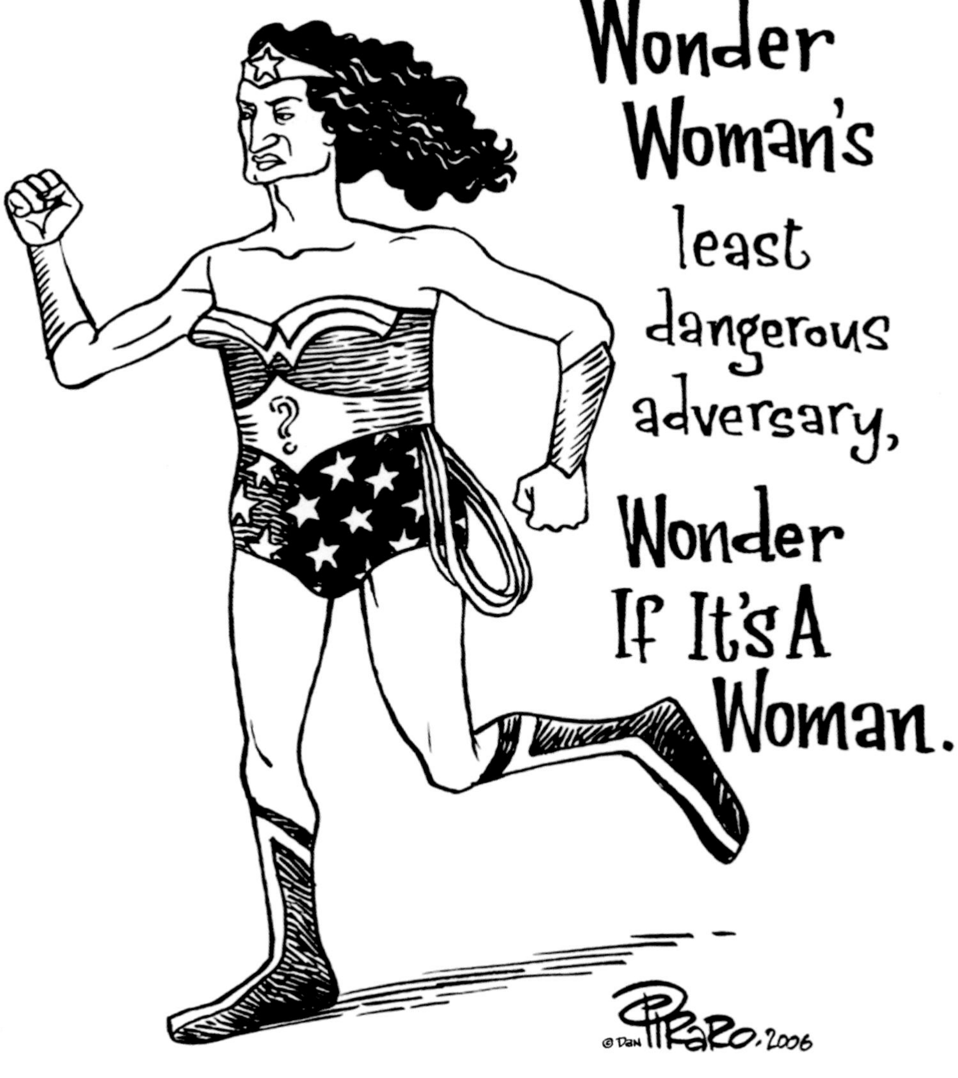
Wonder Woman's least dangerous adversary, Wonder If It's A Woman.
© Dan Piraro. 2006

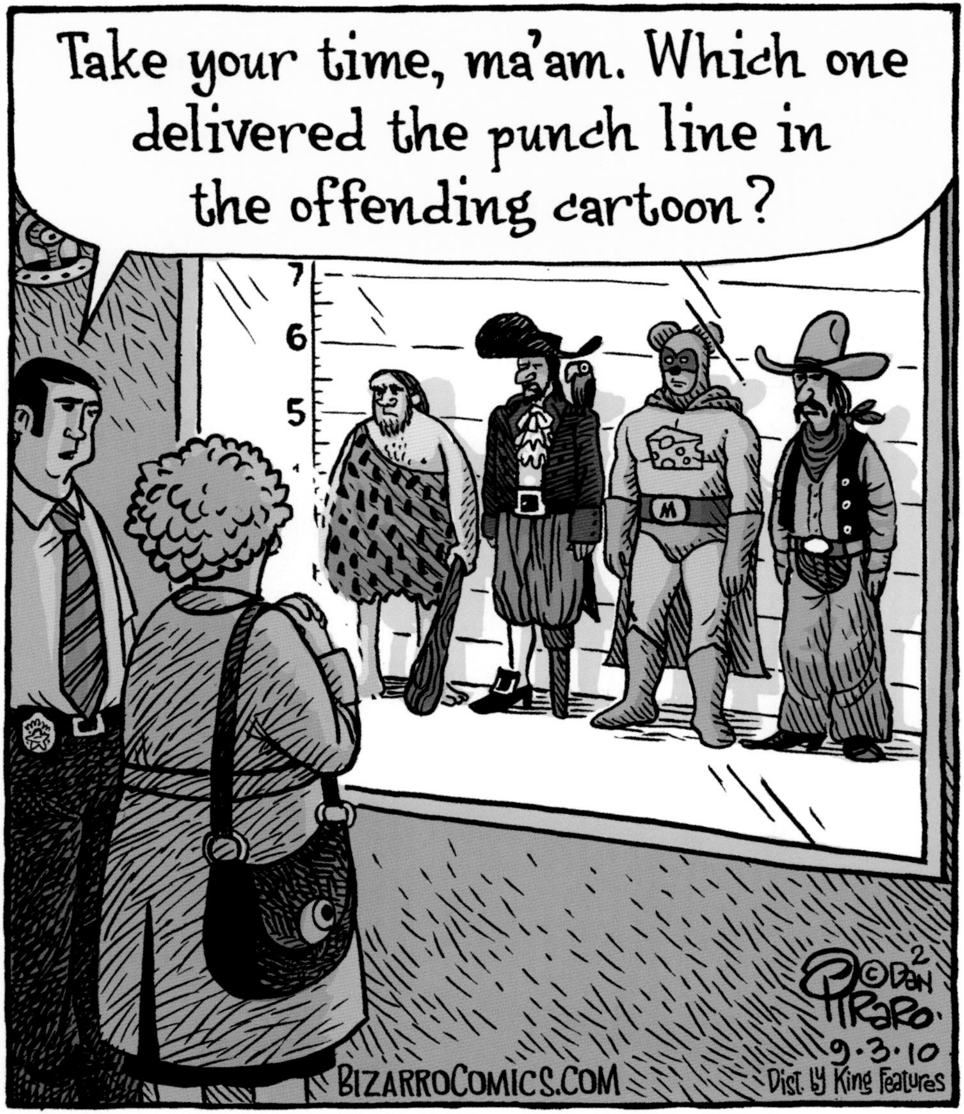
Take your time, ma'am. Which one delivered the punch line in the offending cartoon?
7
6
5
M
©Dan Piraro 9·3·10
BIZARROCOMICS.COM
Dist. by King Features

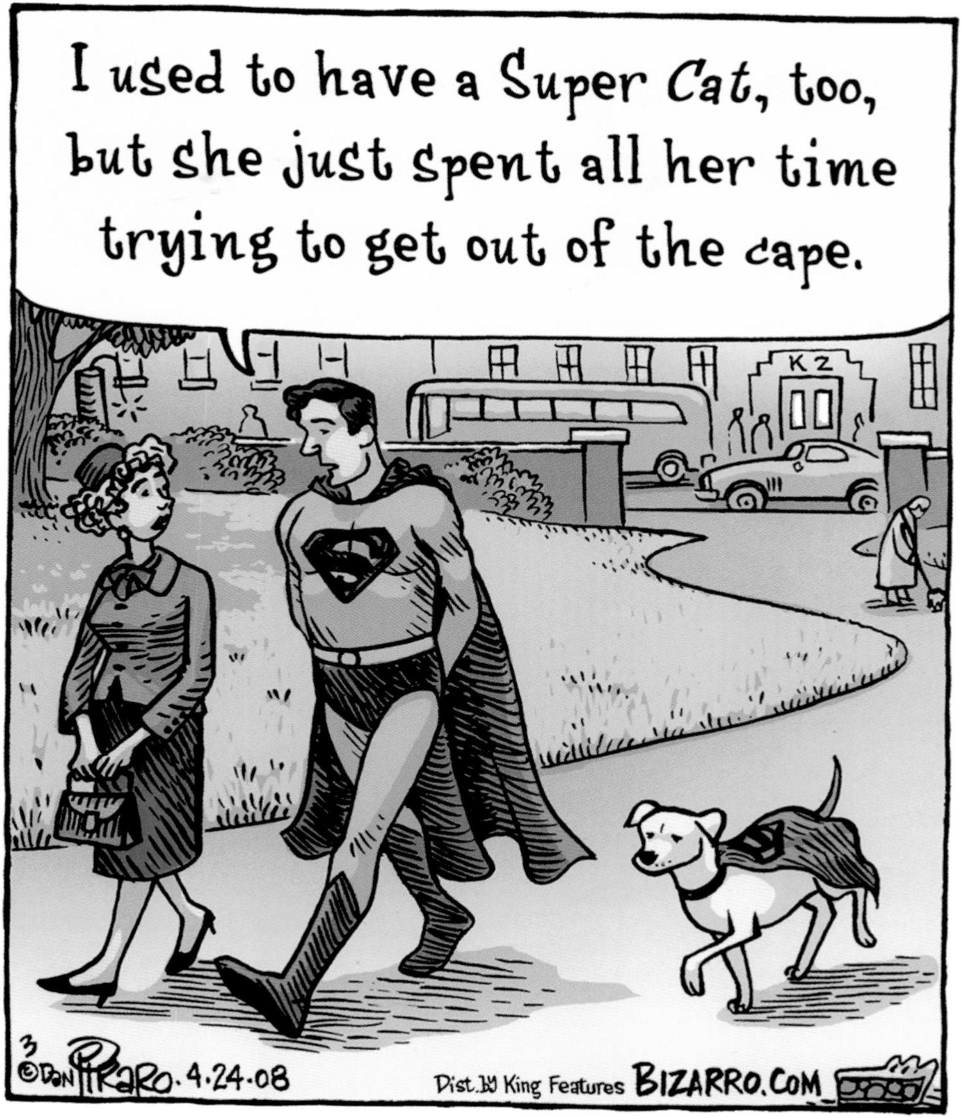
I used to have a Super Cat, too, but she just spent all her time trying to get out of the cape.
KZ
©Dan Piraro 4·24·08
Dist. by King Features BIZARRO.COM

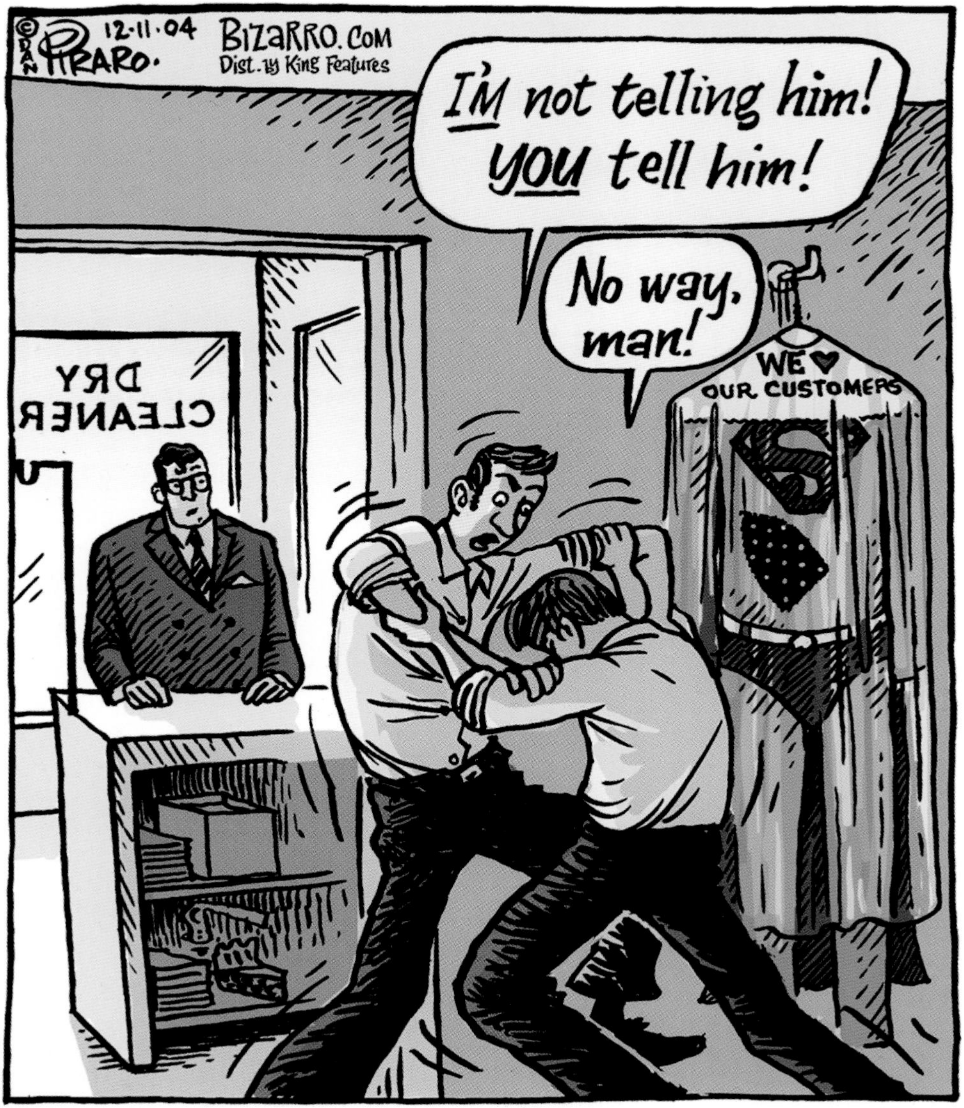
© Dan Piraro. 12-11-04
Bizarro.com
Dist. by King Features
I'M not telling him! YOU tell him!
No way, man!
DRY CLEANER
WE ♥ OUR CUSTOMERS

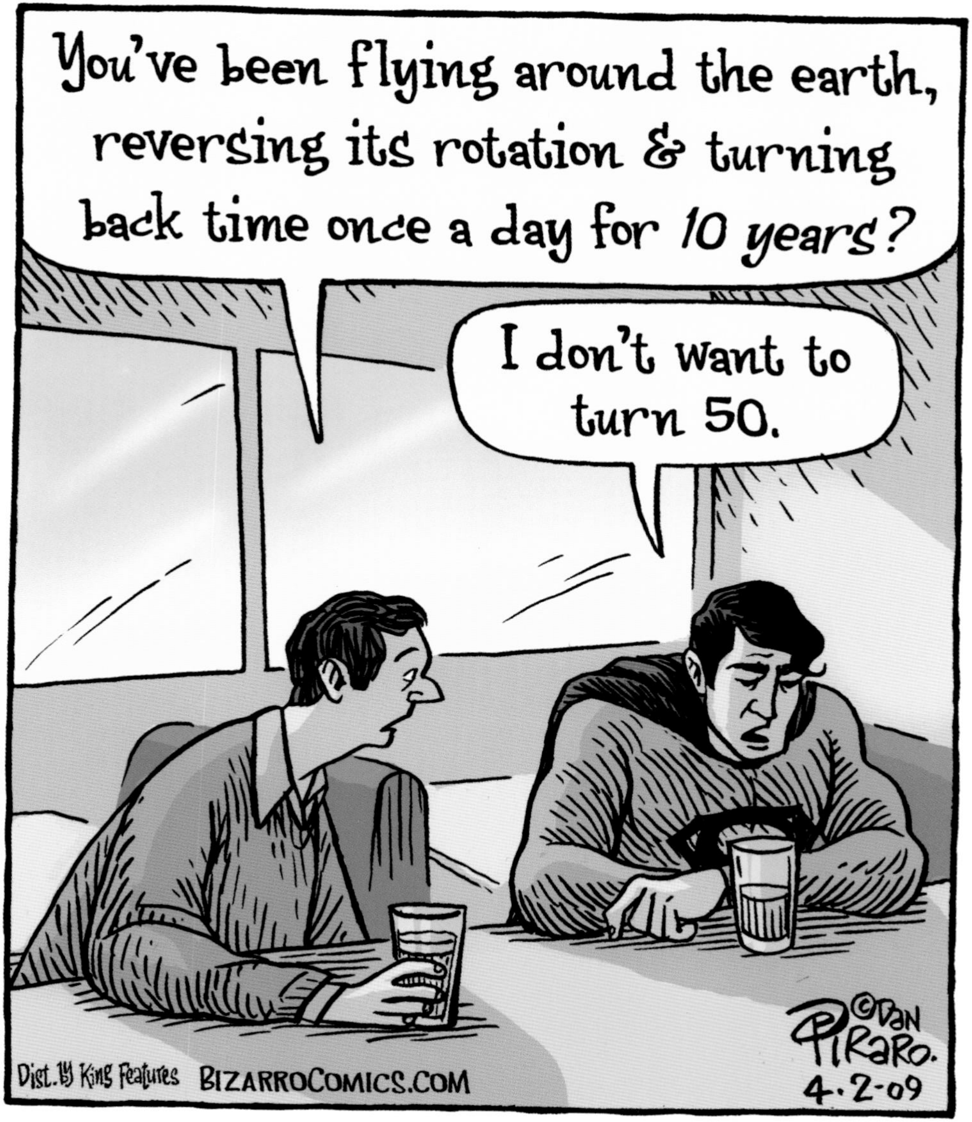
You've been flying around the earth, reversing its rotation & turning back time once a day for 10 years?
I don't want to turn 50.
Dist. by King Features BIZARROCOMICS.COM
©Dan Piraro. 4-2-09

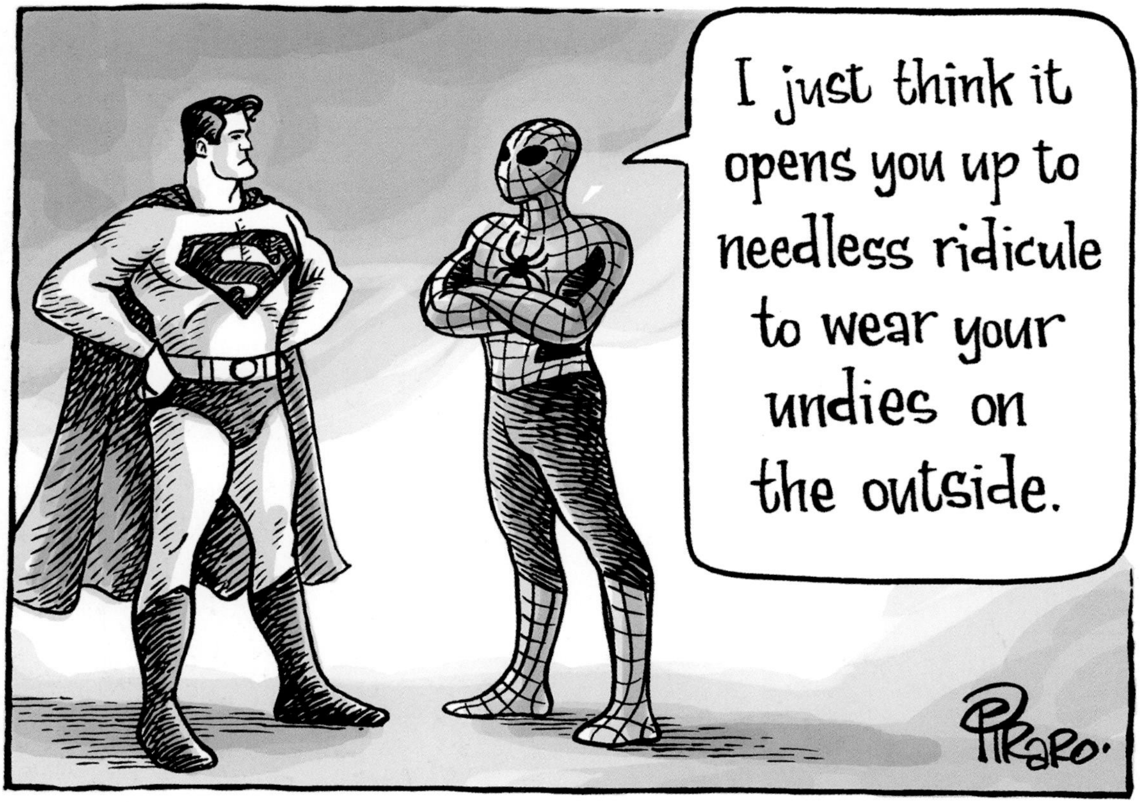
I just think it opens you up to needless ridicule to wear your undies on the outside.
PIRARO.

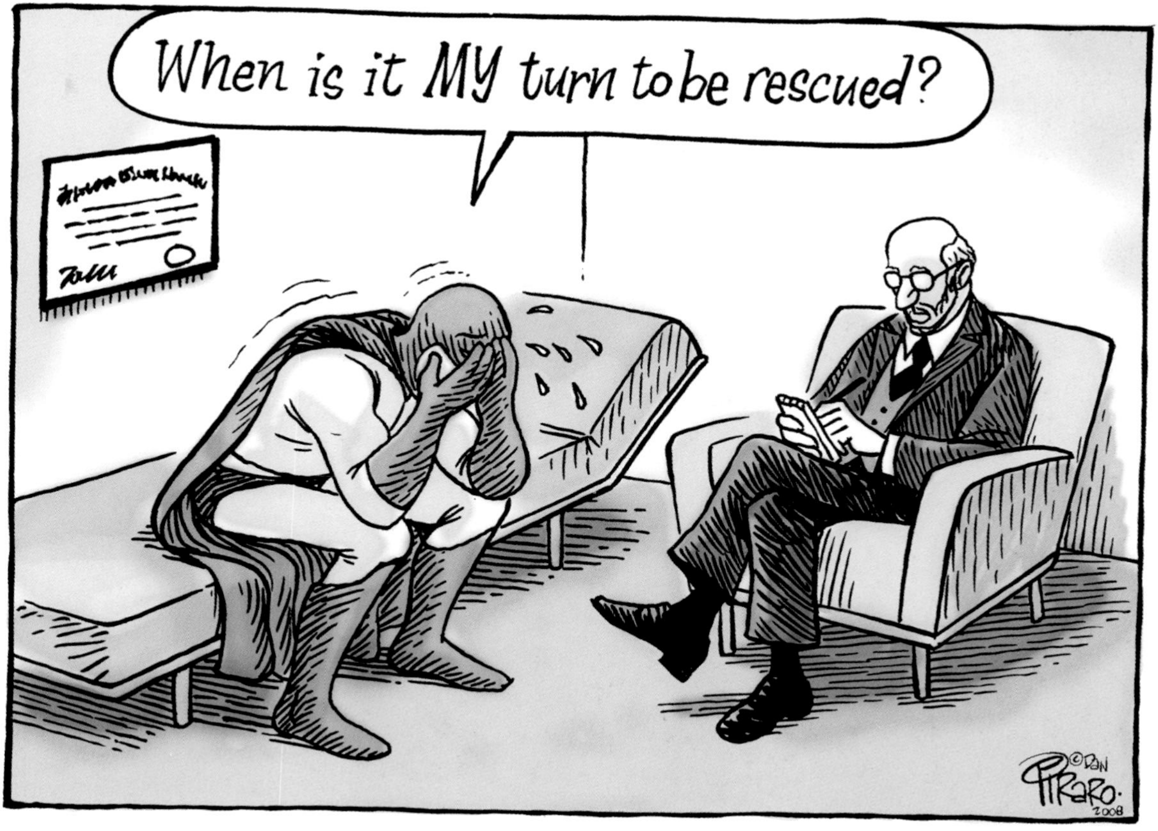
When is it MY turn to be rescued?
©DAN PIRARO 2008

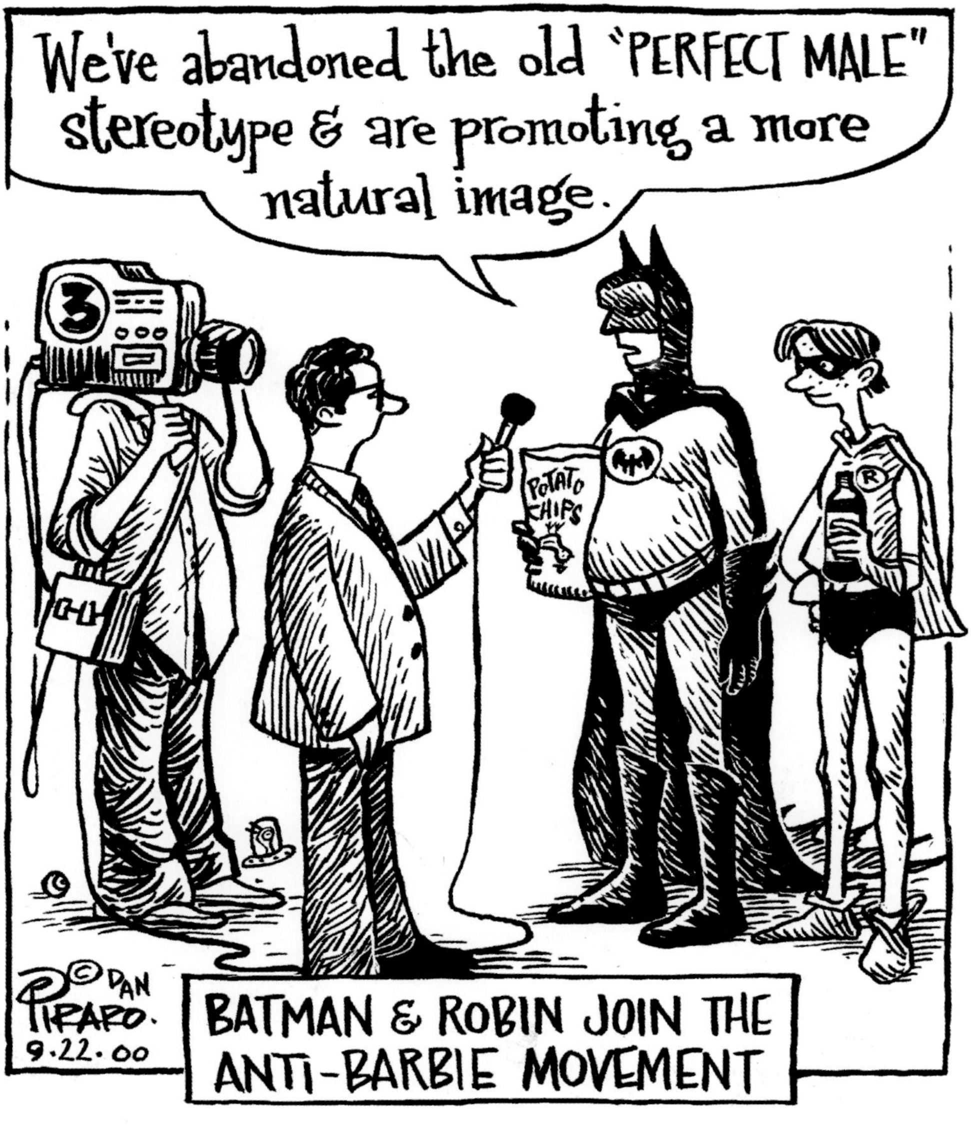
We've abandoned the old "PERFECT MALE" stereotype & are promoting a more natural image.
3
POTATO CHIPS
©DAN PIRARO. 9.22.00
BATMAN & ROBIN JOIN THE ANTI-BARBIE MOVEMENT

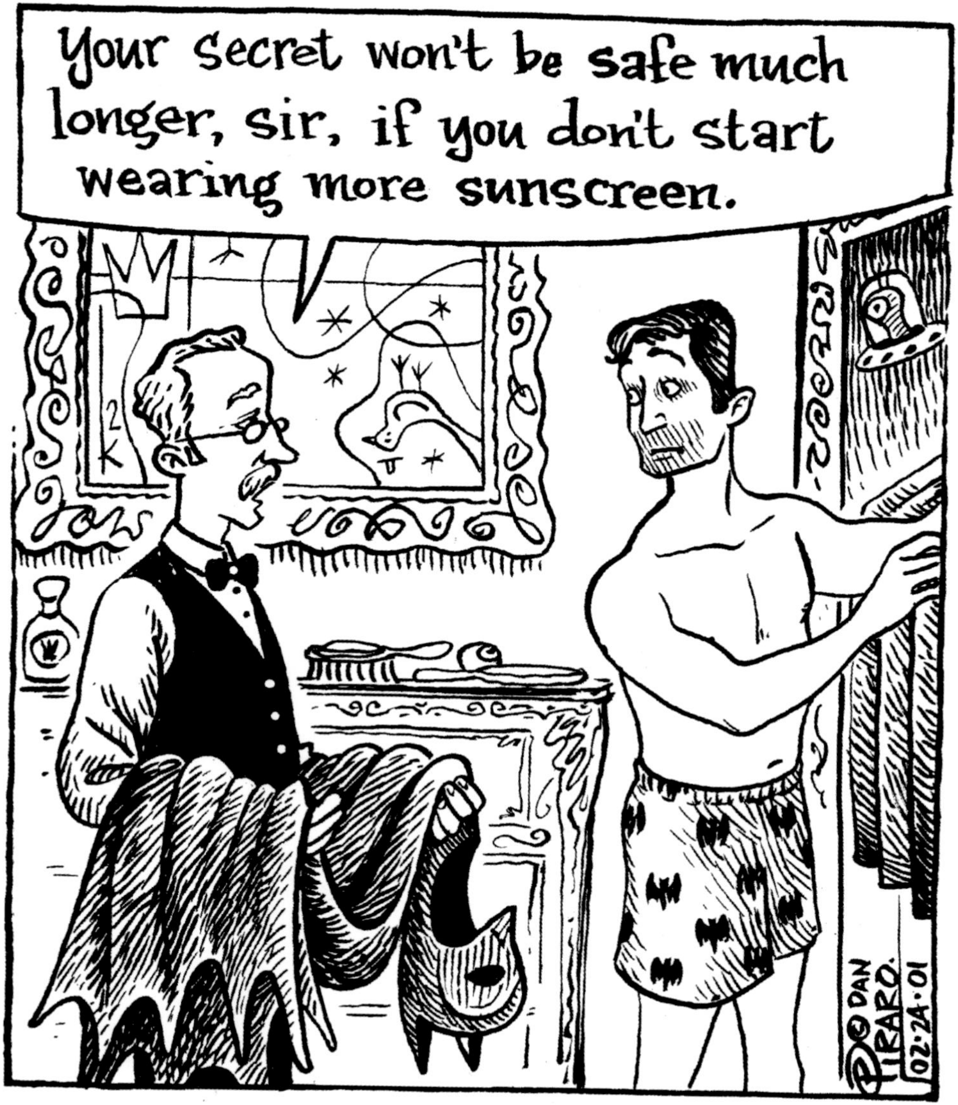
Your secret won't be safe much longer, sir, if you don't start wearing more sunscreen.
© DAN PIRARO. 02·24·01

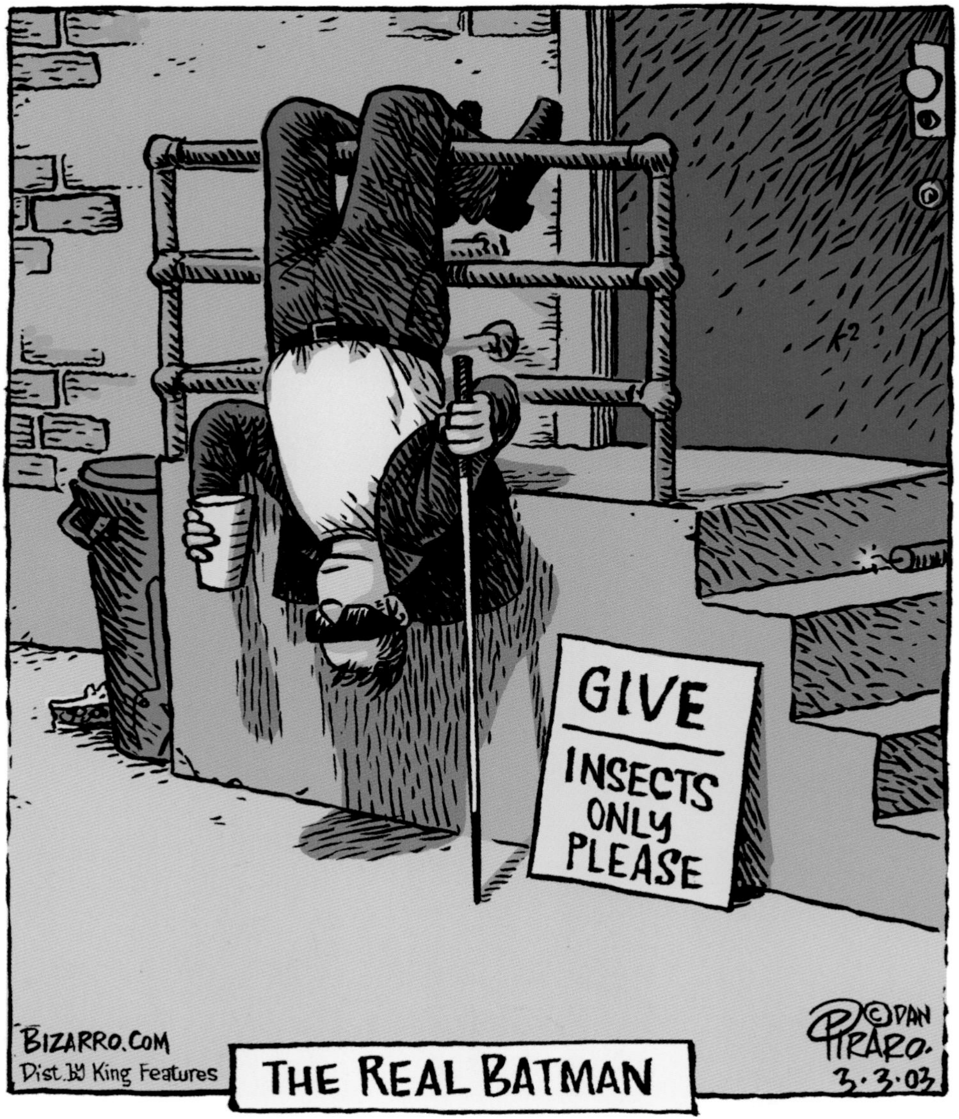
GIVE
INSECTS ONLY PLEASE
BIZARRO.COM
Dist. by King Features
©DAN PIRARO. 3·3·03

THE REAL BATMAN

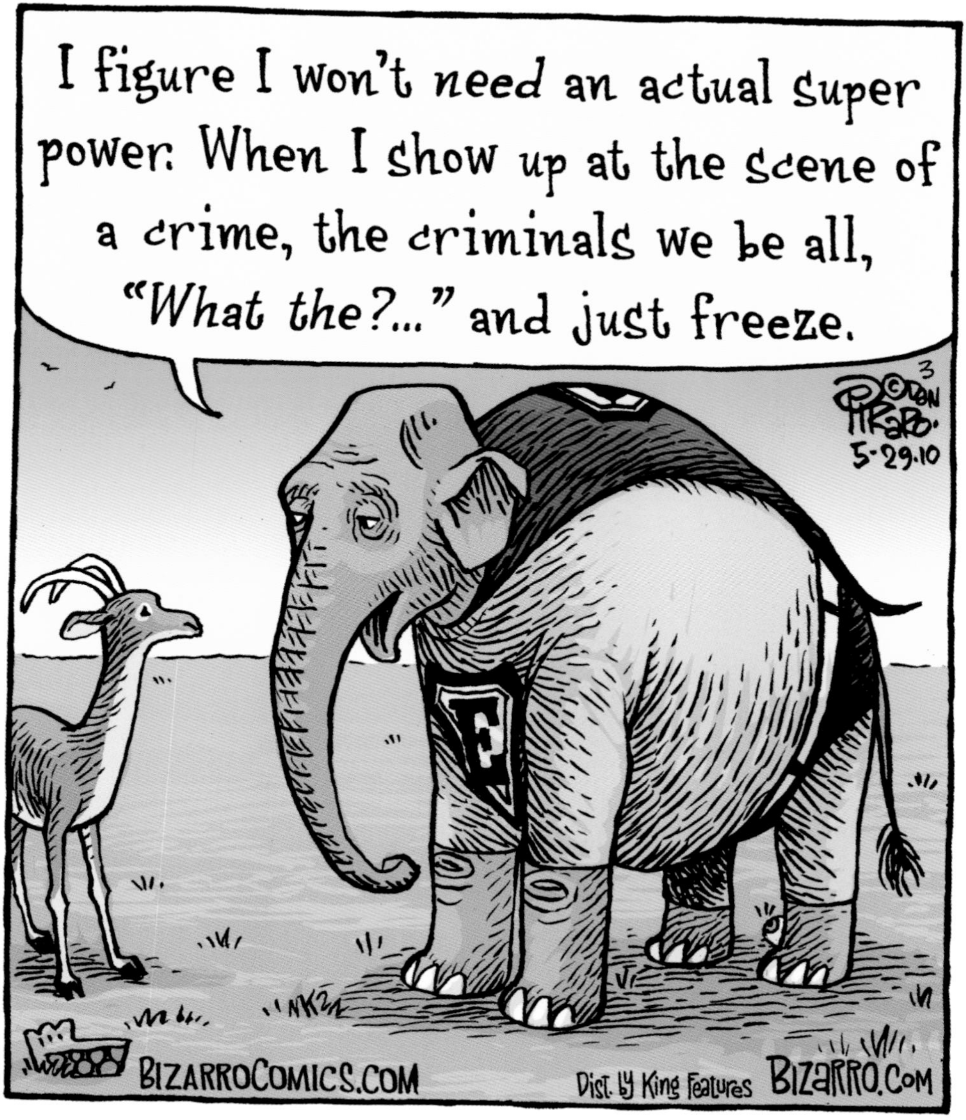
I figure I won't *need* an actual super power. When I show up at the scene of a crime, the criminals we be all, "*What the?...*" and just freeze.
©DON PIRARO 5-29.10
BIZARROCOMICS.COM
Dist. by King Features
BIZARRO.COM

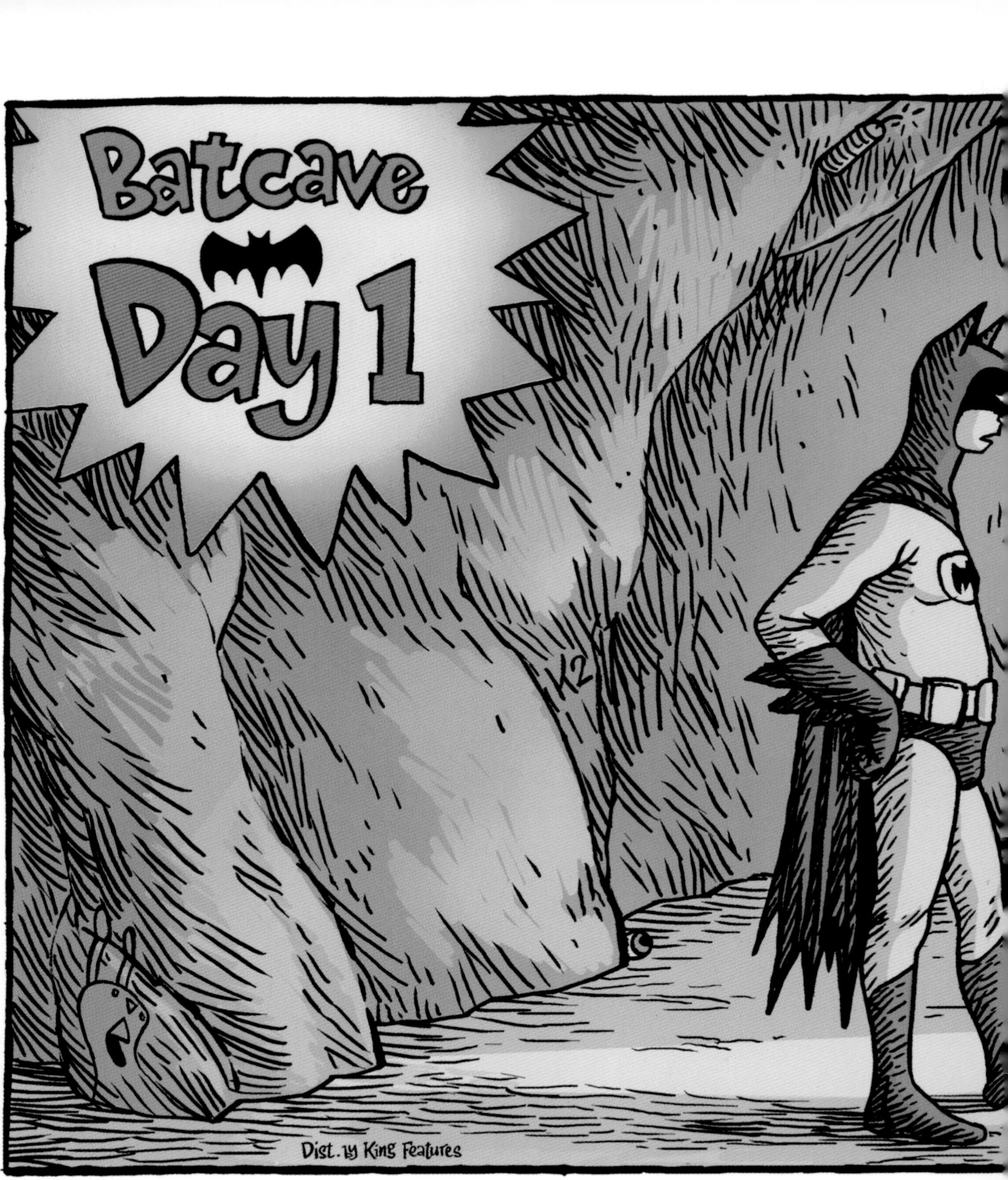
Batcave
Day 1
Dist. by King Features

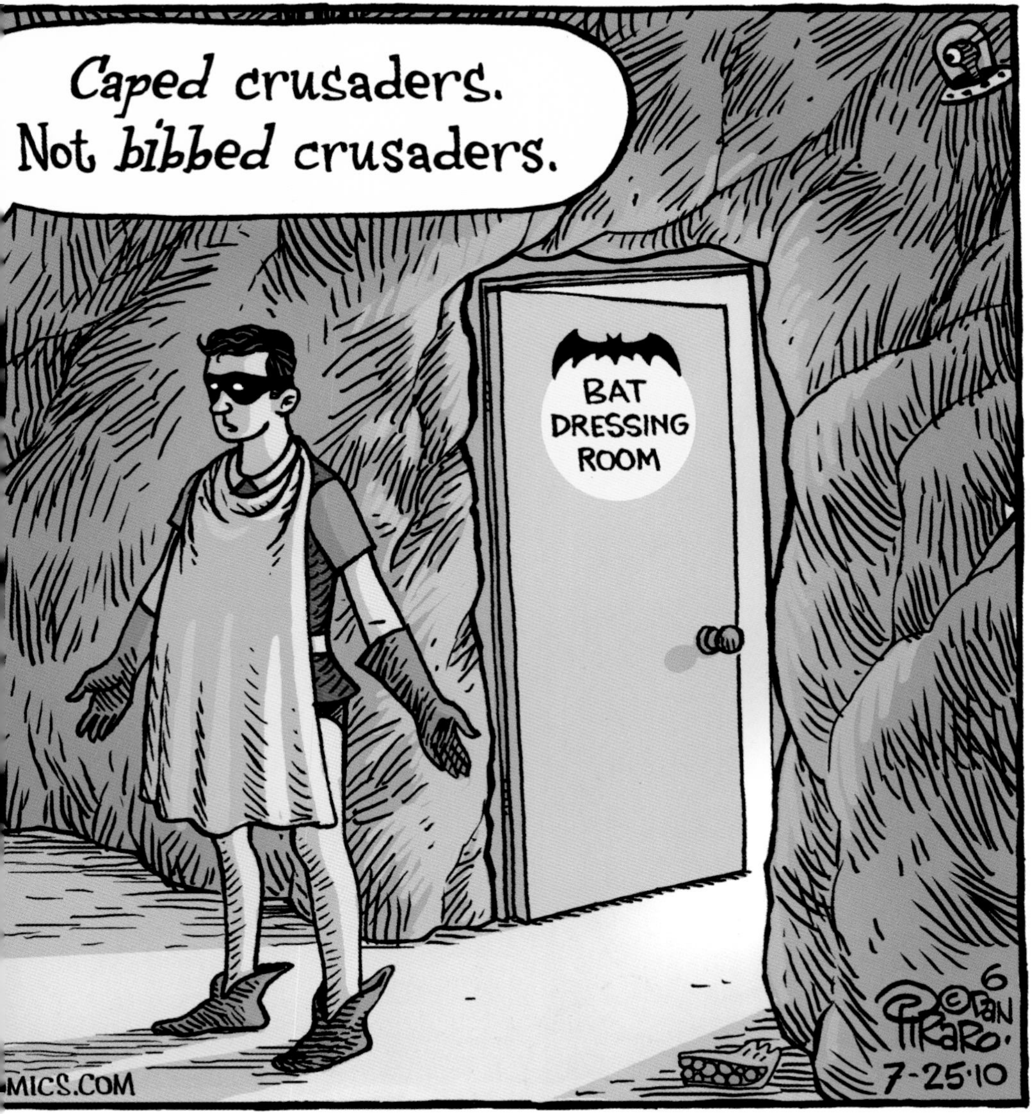
Caped crusaders.
Not bibbed crusaders.
BAT
DRESSING
ROOM
MICS.COM
7-25-10

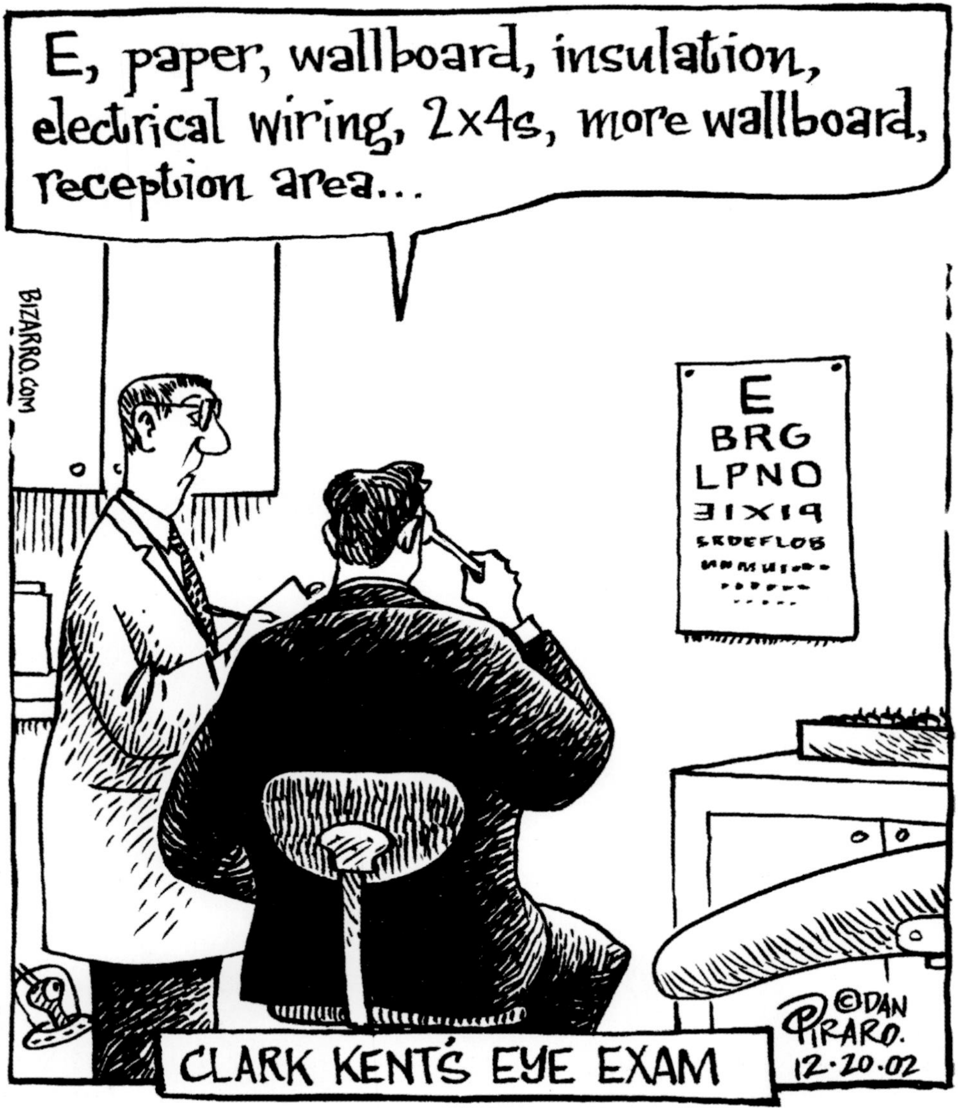
E, paper, wallboard, insulation, electrical wiring, 2x4s, more wallboard, reception area...
BIZARRO.COM
E
BRG
LPNO
©DAN PIRARO. 12·20·02
CLARK KENT'S EYE EXAM

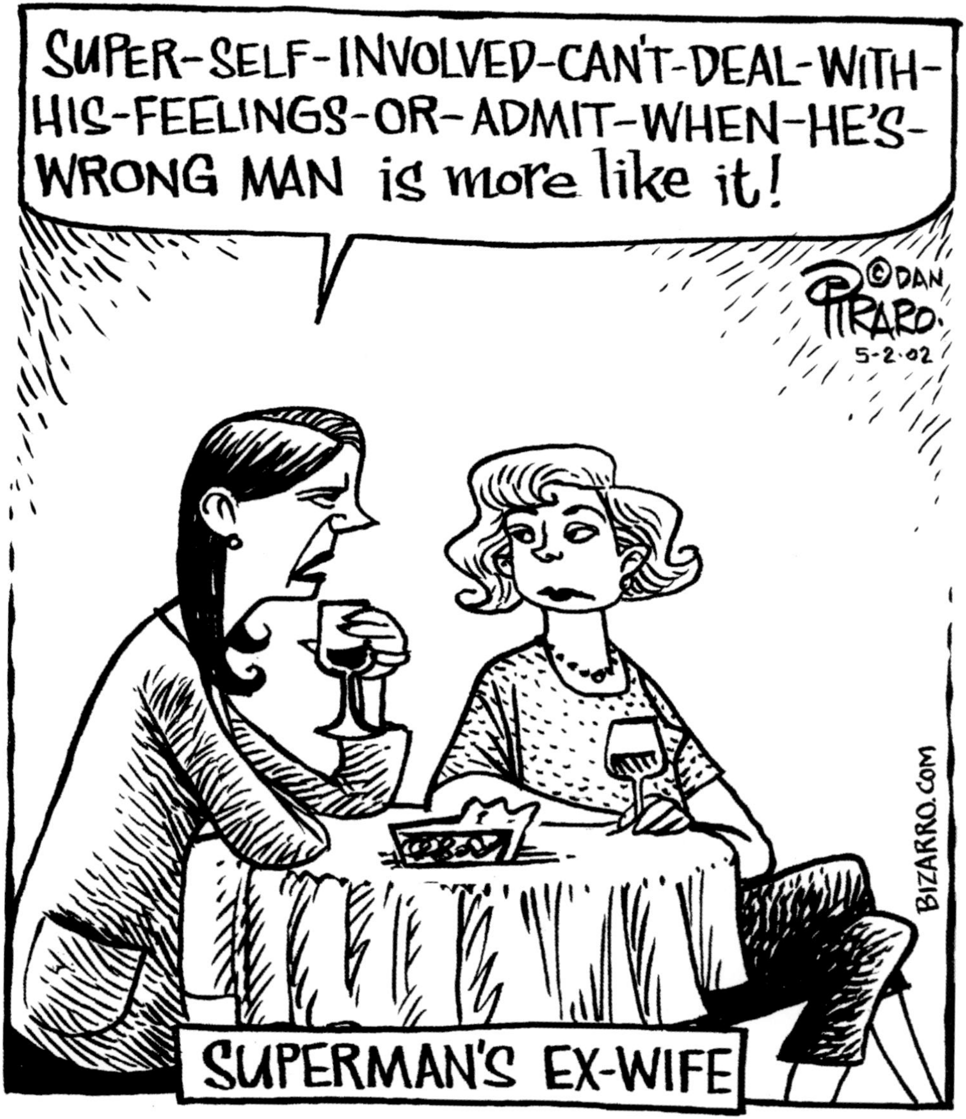
SUPER-SELF-INVOLVED-CAN'T-DEAL-WITH-HIS-FEELINGS-OR-ADMIT-WHEN-HE'S-WRONG MAN is more like it!
©DAN PIRARO 5-2-02
BIZARRO.COM
SUPERMAN'S EX-WIFE

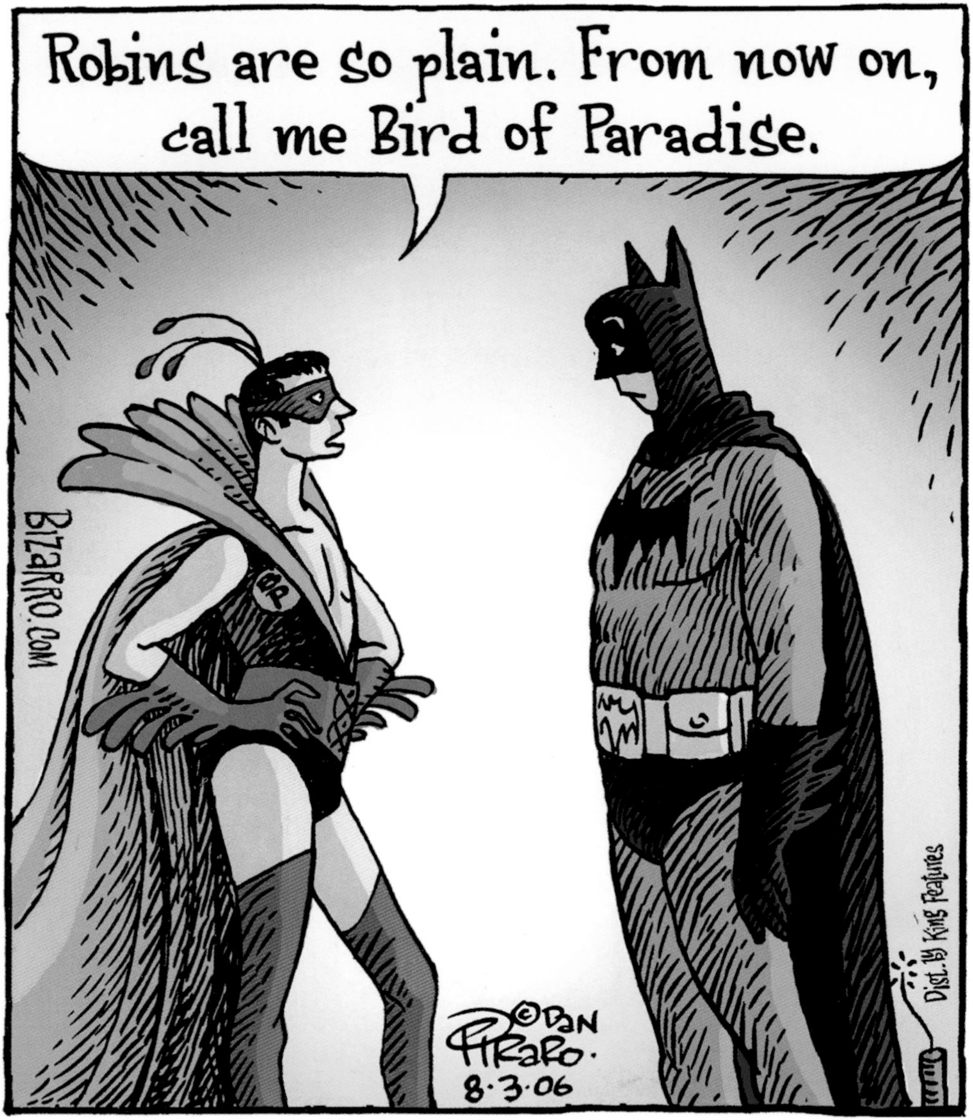
Robins are so plain. From now on, call me Bird of Paradise.
BIZARRO.COM
©DAN PIRARO. 8·3·06
Dist. by King Features

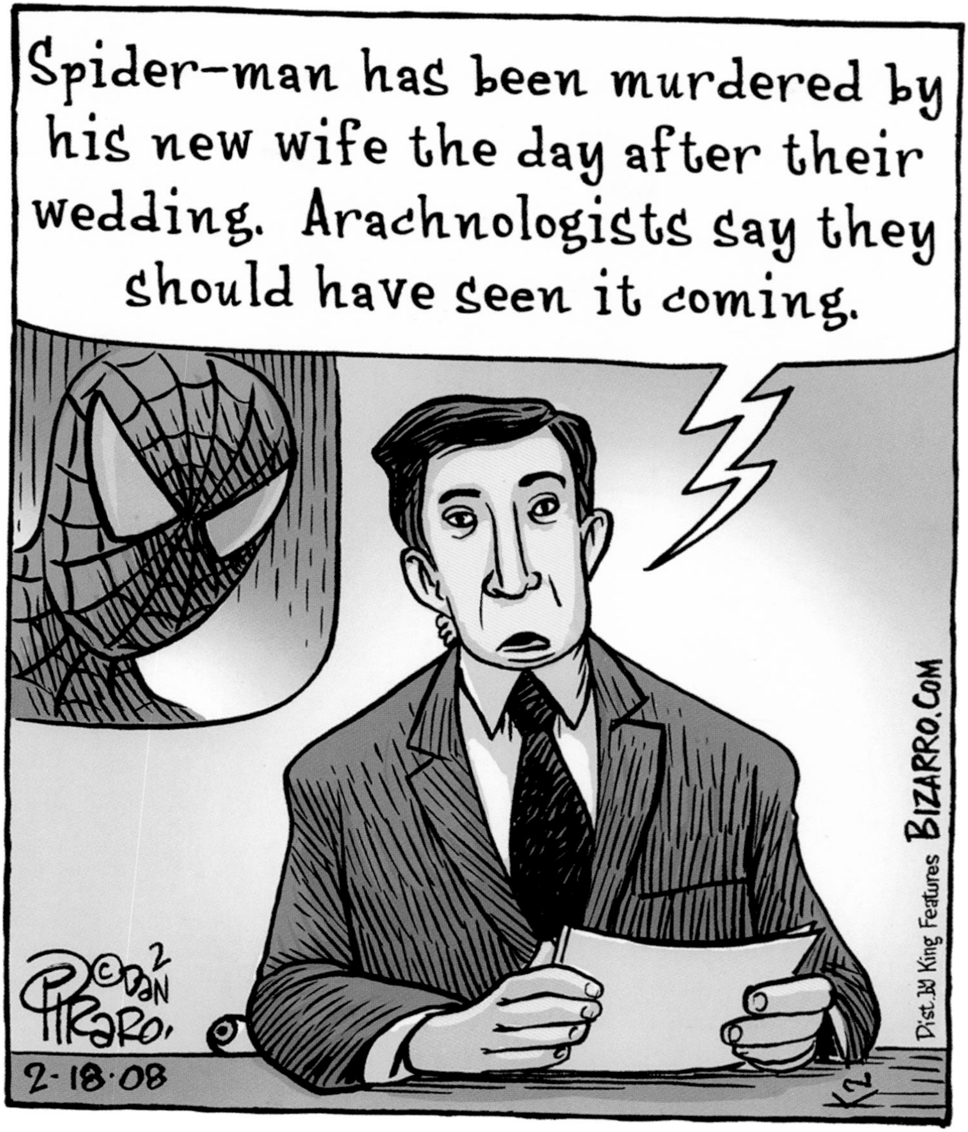
Spider-man has been murdered by his new wife the day after their wedding. Arachnologists say they should have seen it coming.
©2 DAN PIRARO, 2-18-08
Dist. by King Features BIZARRO.COM

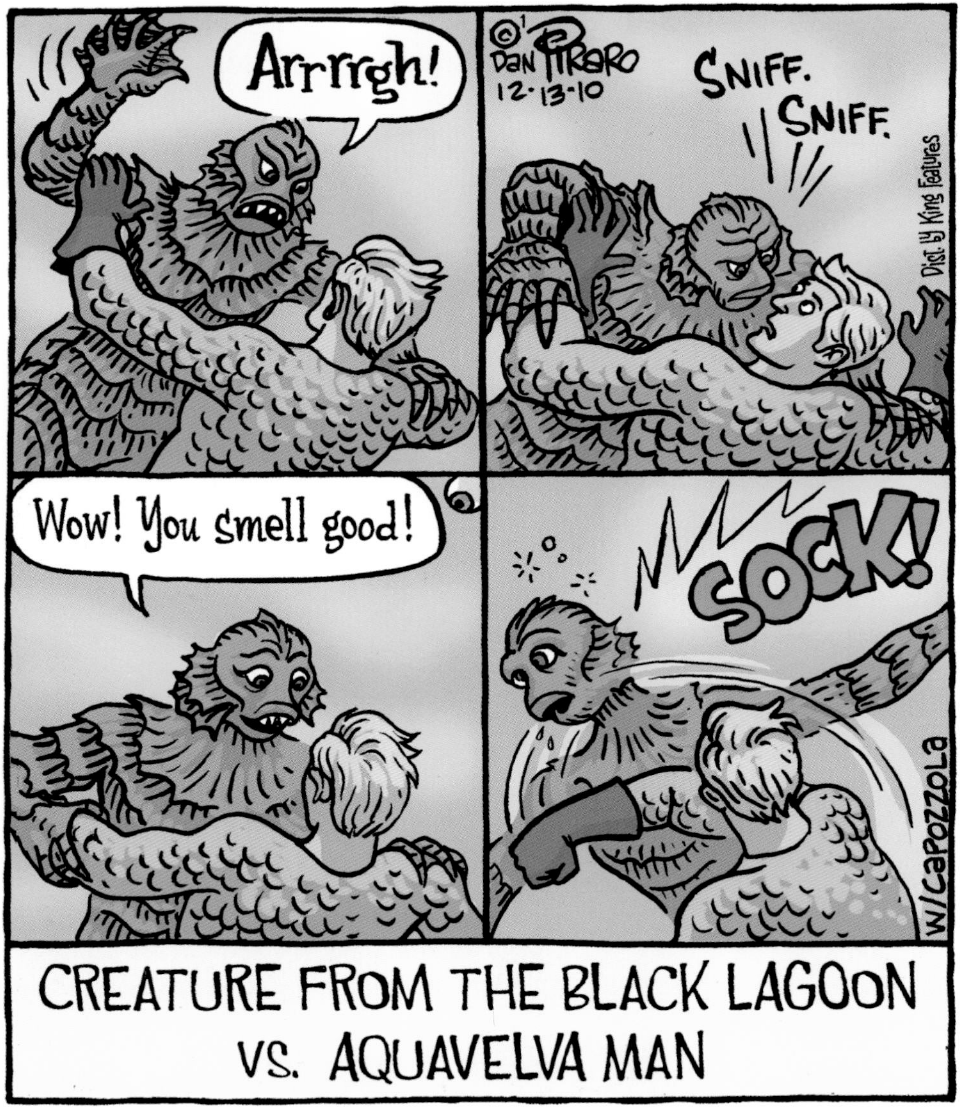
Arrrrgh!
© Dan Piraro 12-13-10
Dist. by King Features
SNIFF. SNIFF.
Wow! You smell good!
SOCK!
w/Capozzola
CREATURE FROM THE BLACK LAGOON
VS. AQUAVELVA MAN

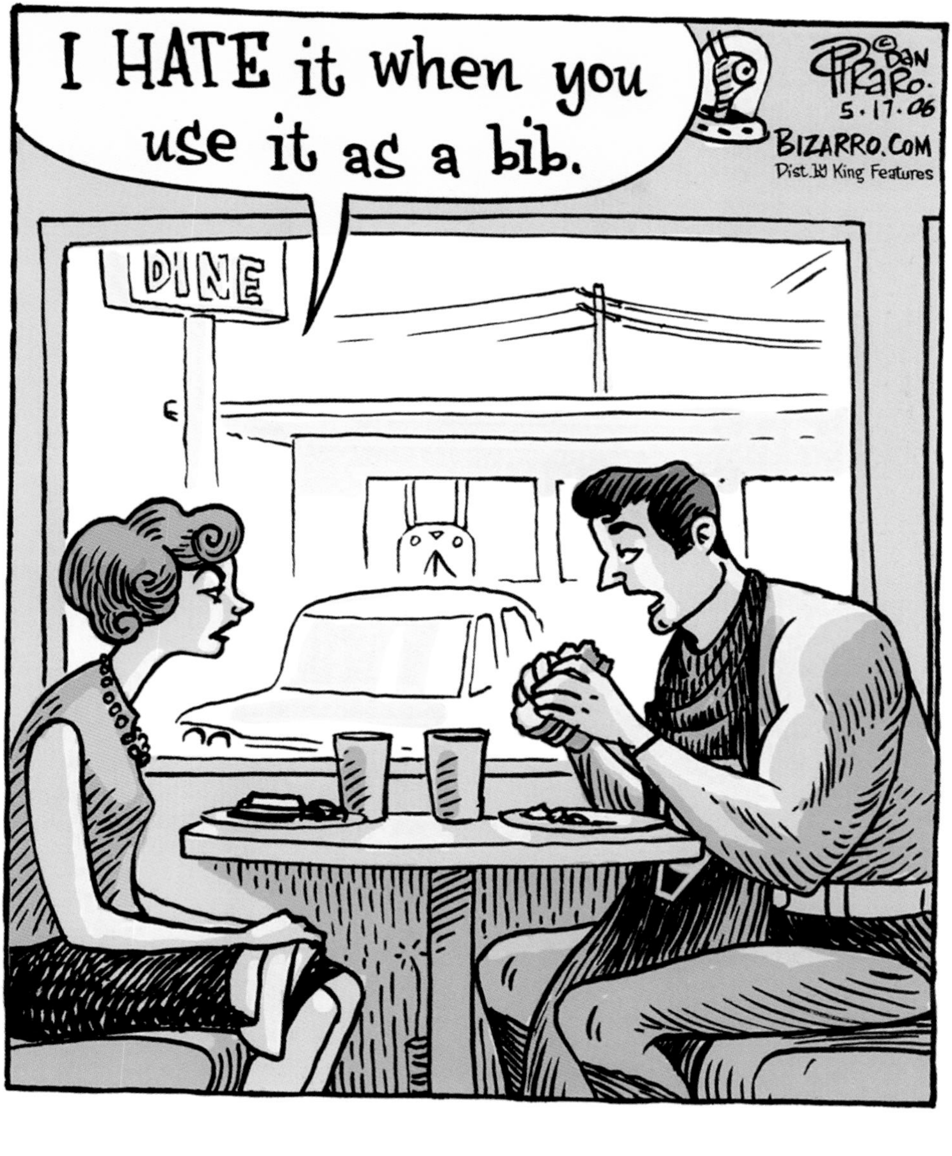
I HATE it when you use it as a bib.
DINE
© DAN PIRARO 5.17.06
BIZARRO.COM
Dist. by King Features

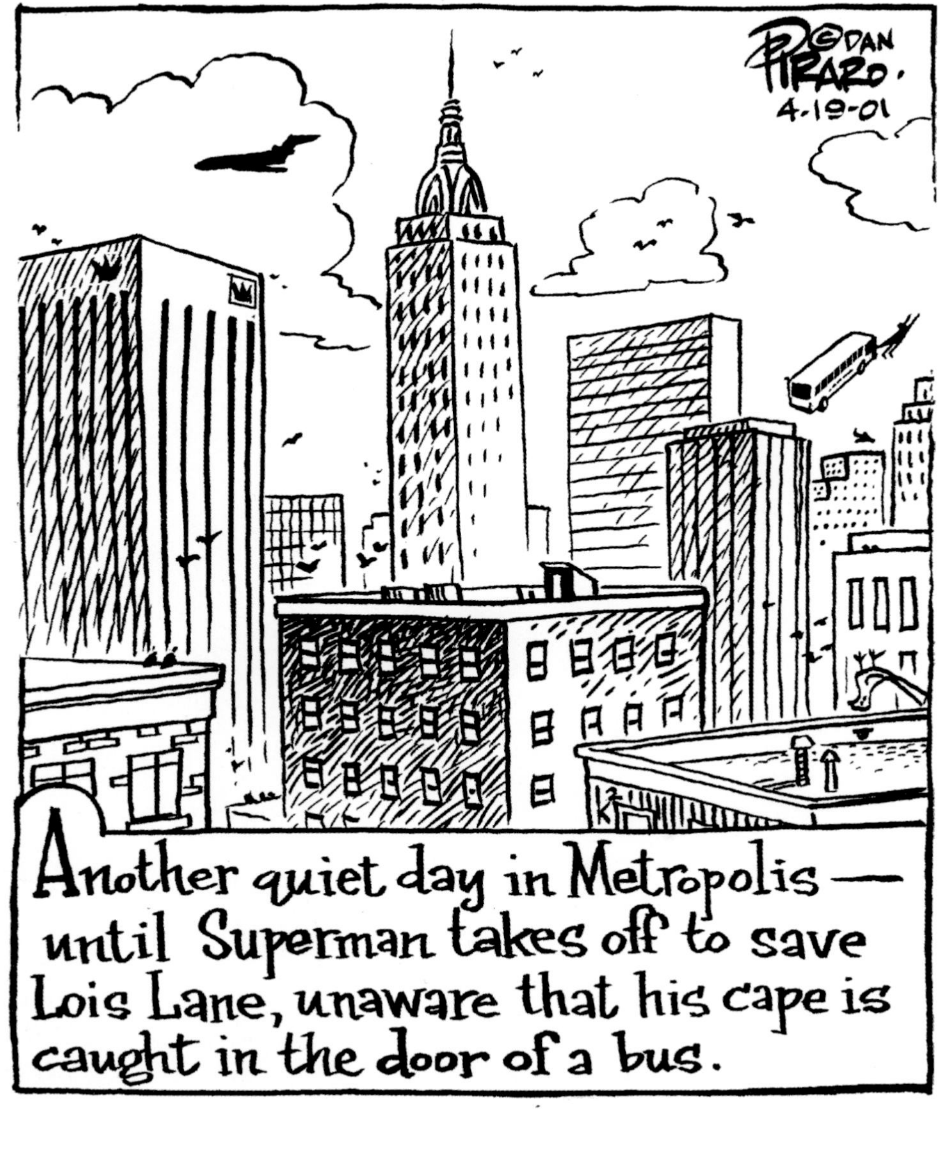
©DAN PIRARO.
4-19-01

Another quiet day in Metropolis — until Superman takes off to save Lois Lane, unaware that his cape is caught in the door of a bus.

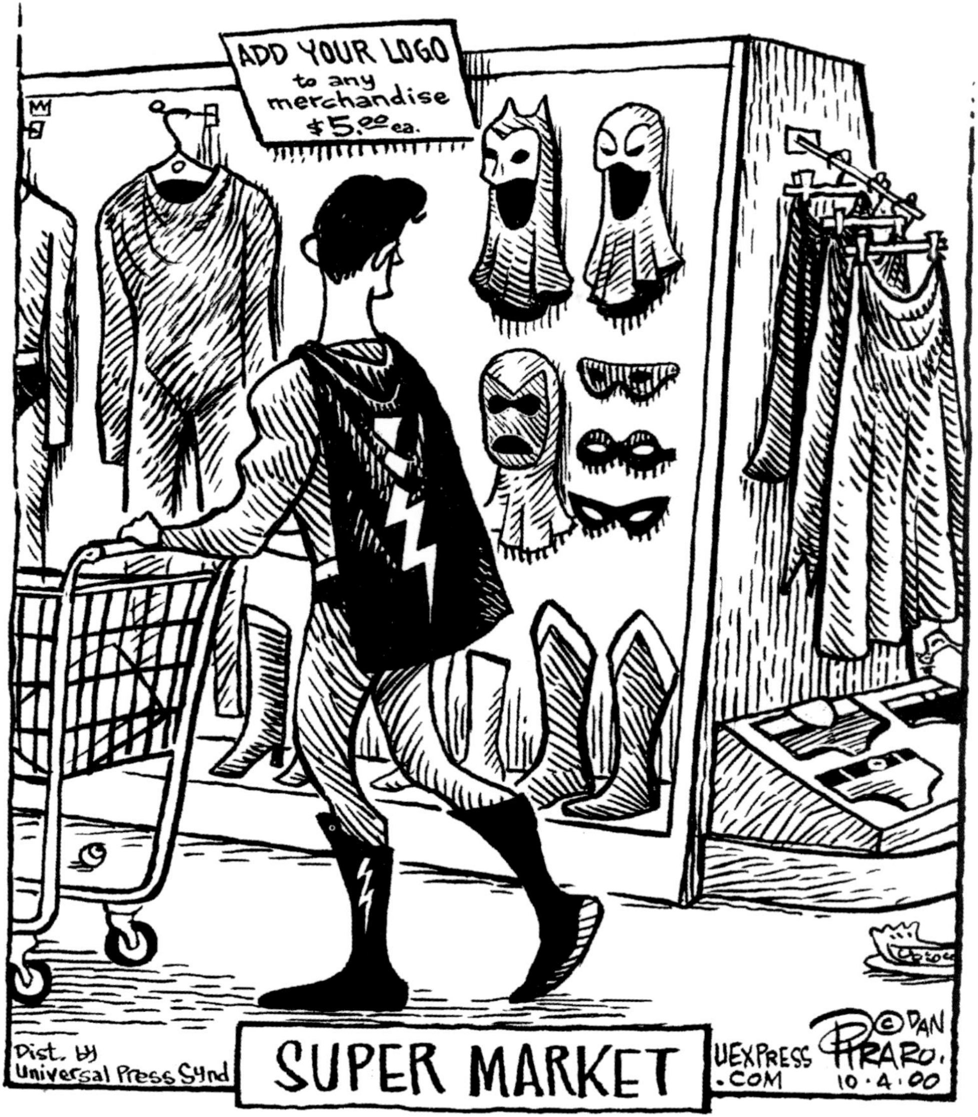
ADD YOUR LOGO to any merchandise $5.00 ea.
Dist. by Universal Press Synd
SUPER MARKET
UEXPRESS .COM
© DAN PIRARO. 10·4·00

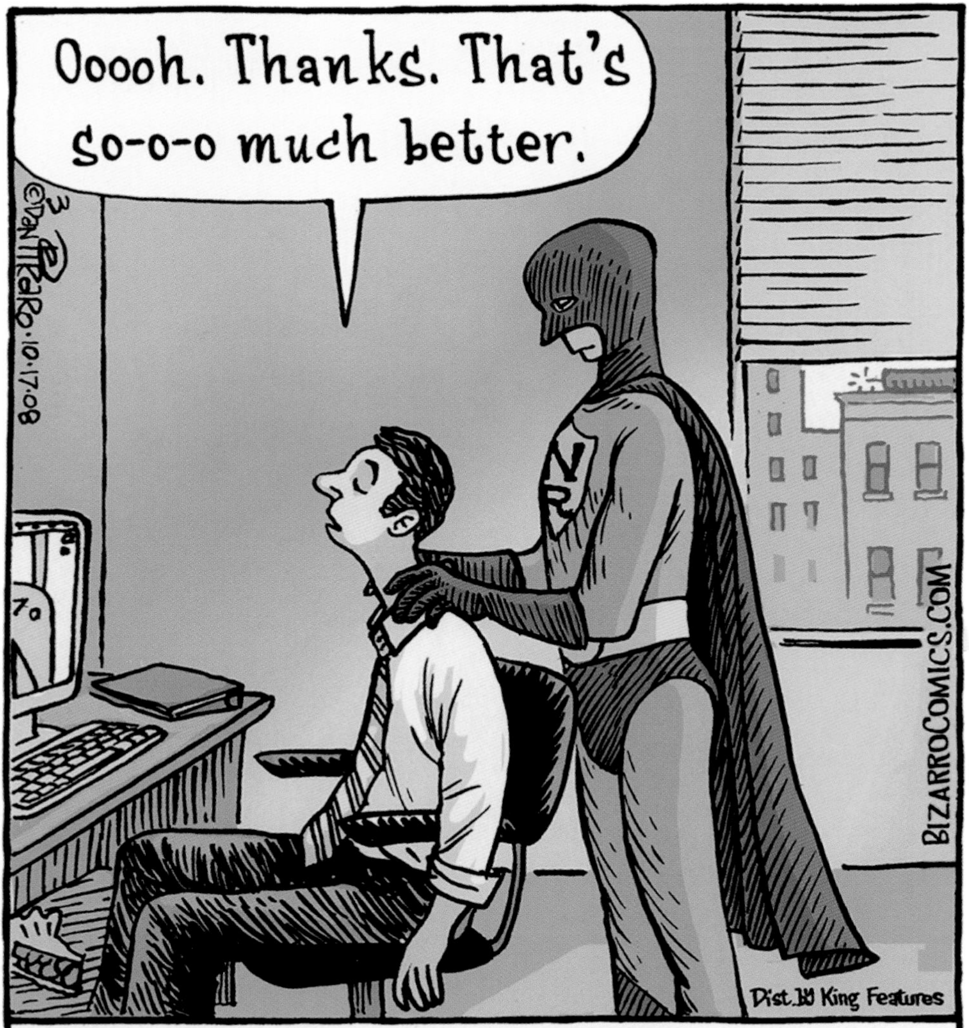
Ooooh. Thanks. That's so-o-o much better.
©Dan Piraro 10.17.08
BIZARROCOMICS.COM
Dist. by King Features
CAPTAIN NECK RUB SAVES THE DAY

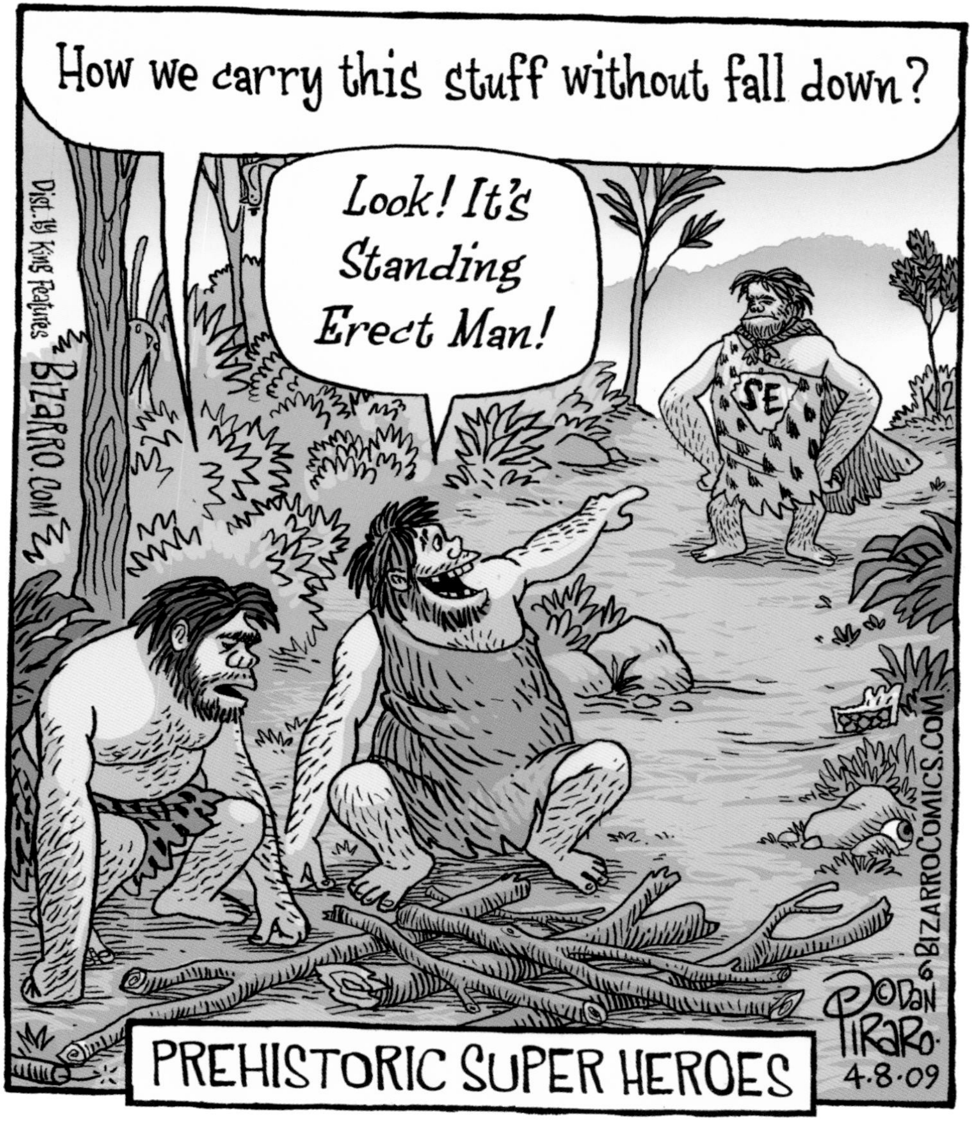
How we carry this stuff without fall down?
Look! It's Standing Erect Man!
SE
PREHISTORIC SUPER HEROES
Dist. by King Features
BIZARRO.COM
©BIZARROCOMICS.COM
©DAN PIRARO 4.8.09

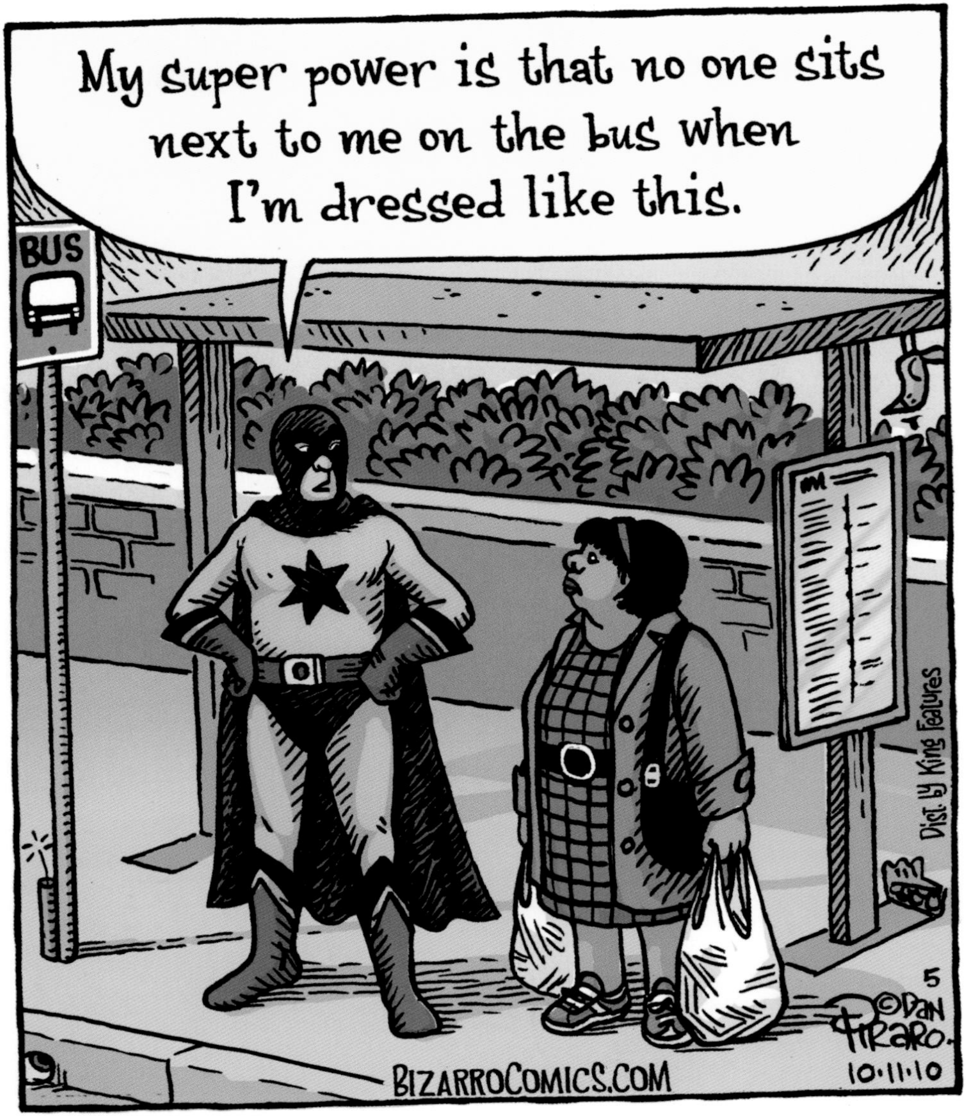
My super power is that no one sits next to me on the bus when I'm dressed like this.
BUS
Dist. by King Features
5
©DAN PIRARO.
10·11·10
BIZARROCOMICS.COM

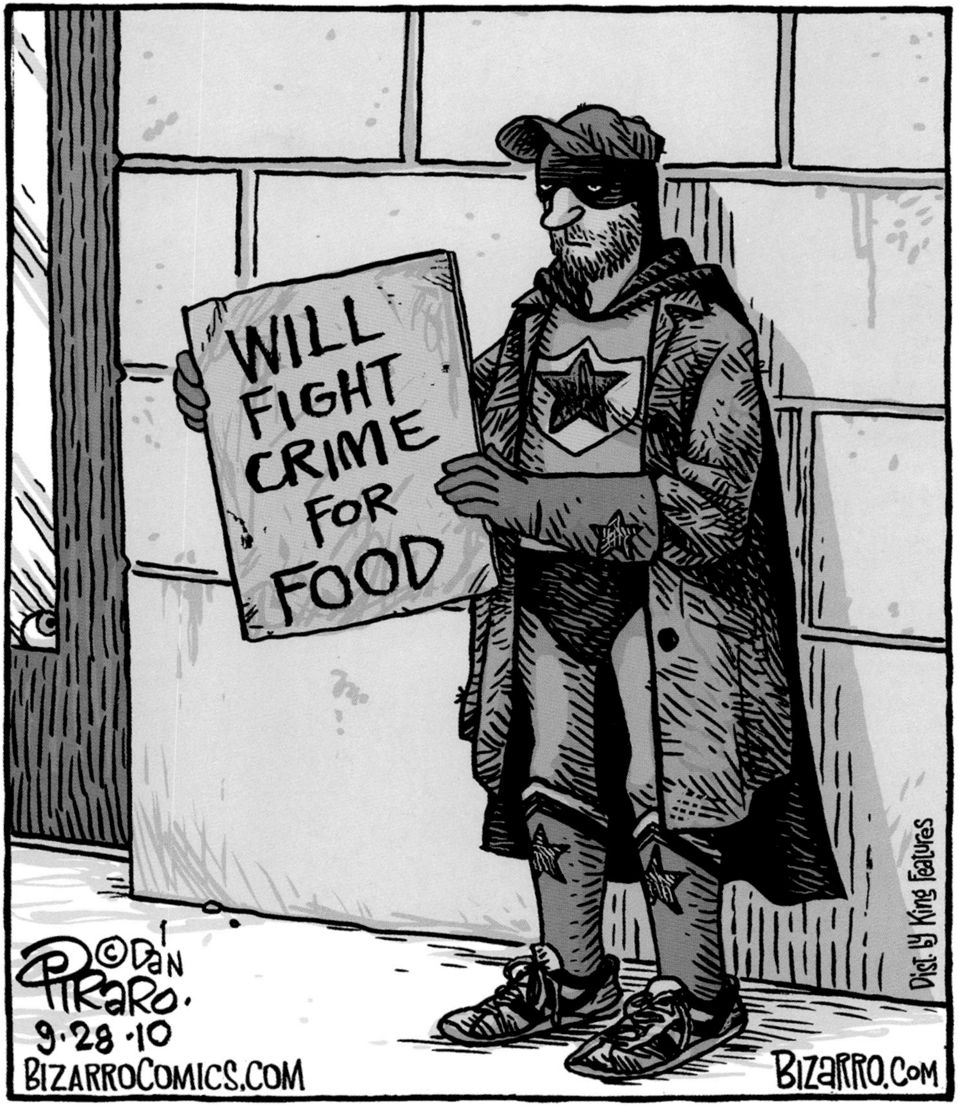
WILL FIGHT CRIME FOR FOOD
©DAN PIRARO. 9·28·10
BIZARROCOMICS.COM
BIZARRO.COM
Dist. by King Features

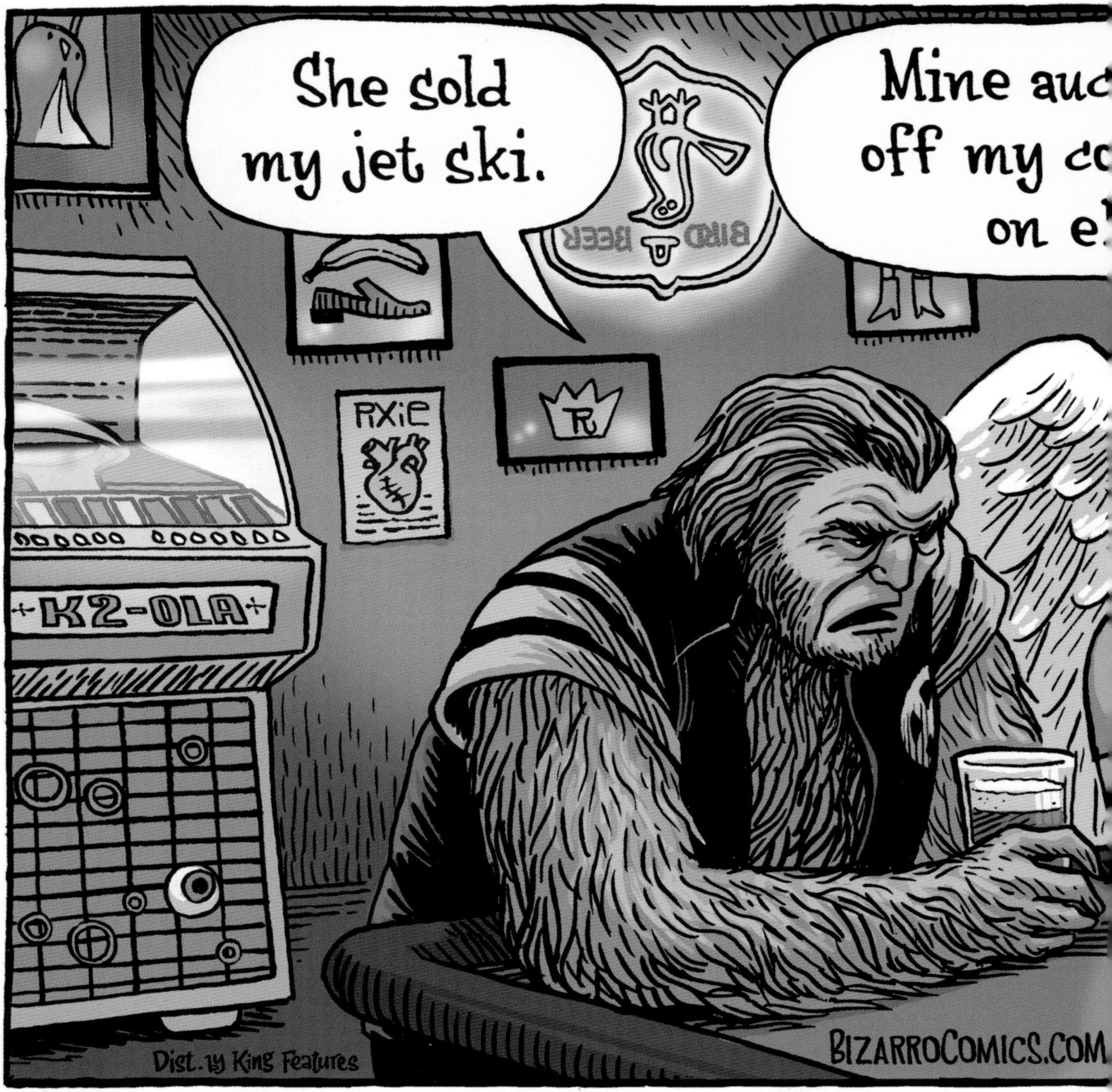
She sold my jet ski.
Mine
off my
on
PiXiE
K2-OLA
Dist. by King Features
BIZARROCOMICS.COM

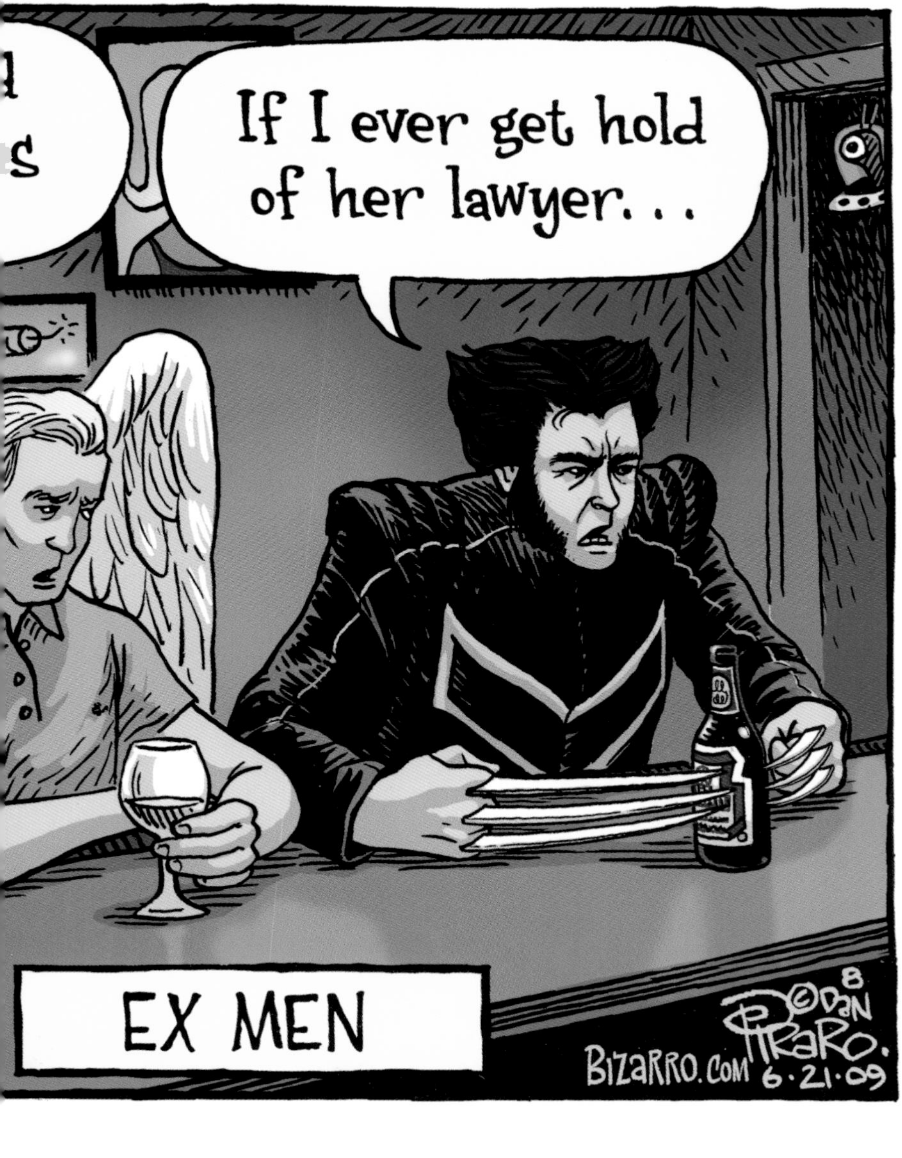
If I ever get hold of her lawyer. . .
© DAN PIRARO
BIZARRO.COM
6·21·09
EX MEN

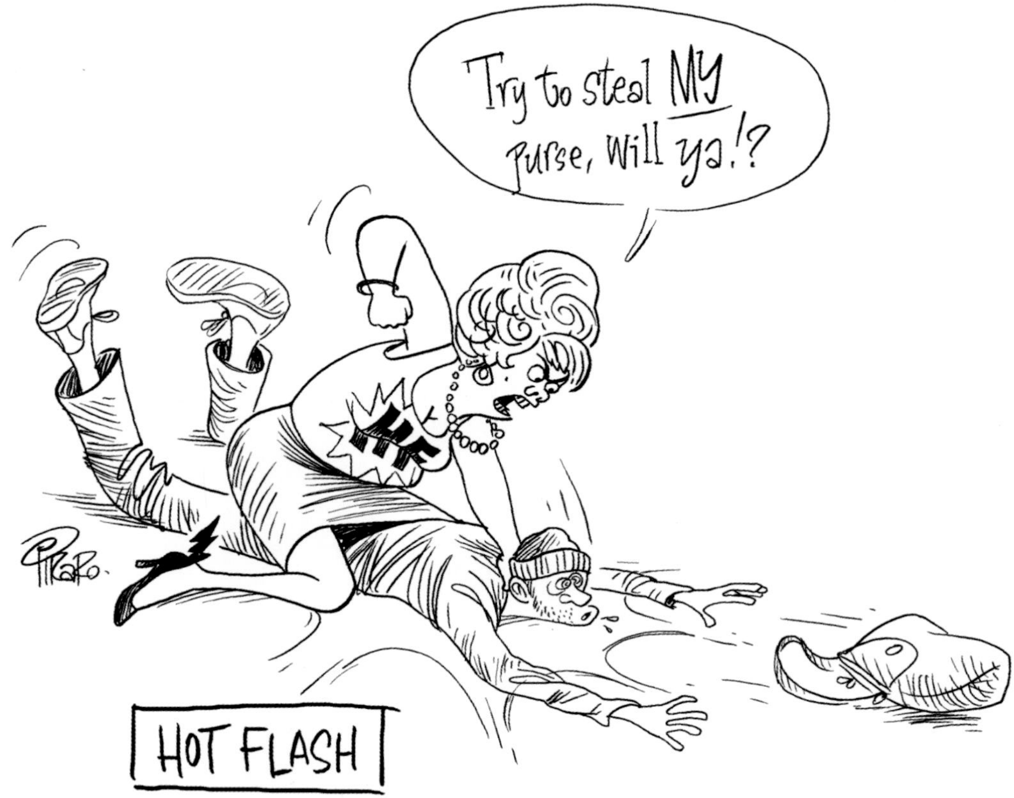
Try to steal MY purse, will ya!?
HOT FLASH
PIRARO.

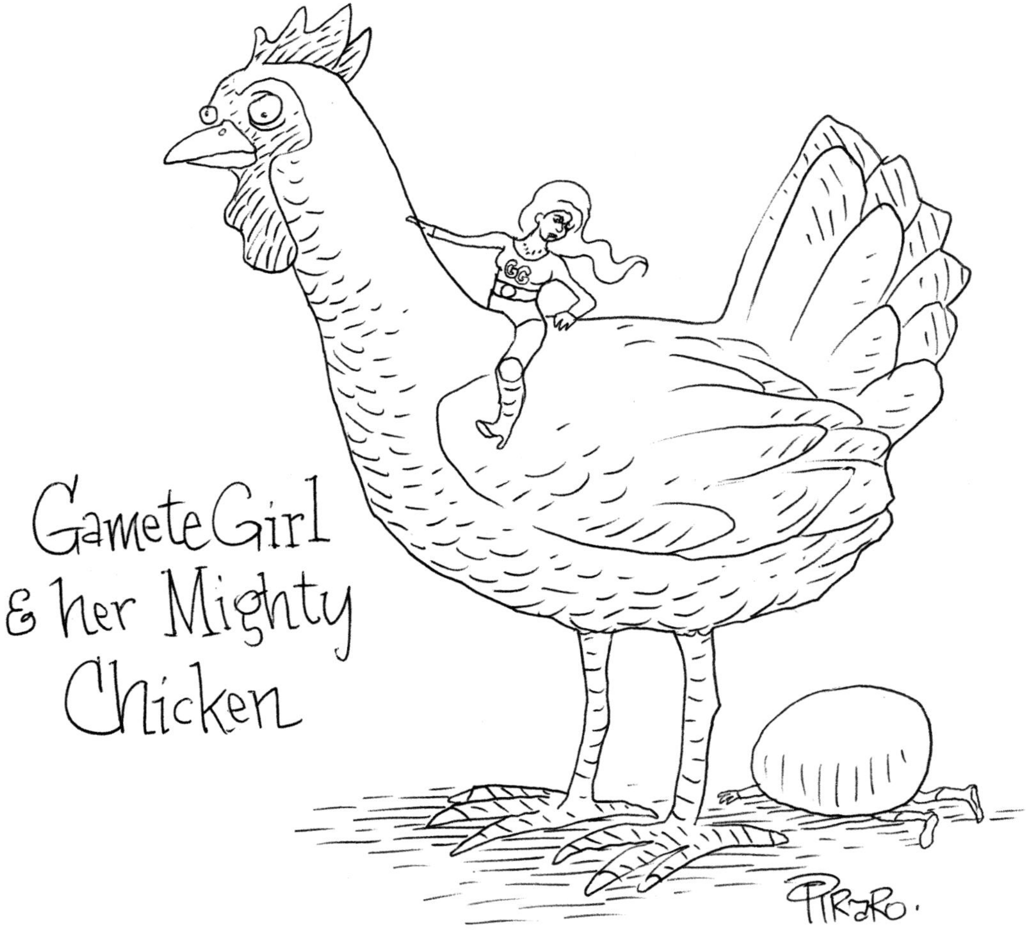
Gamete Girl
& her Mighty
Chicken
GG
PIRARO.

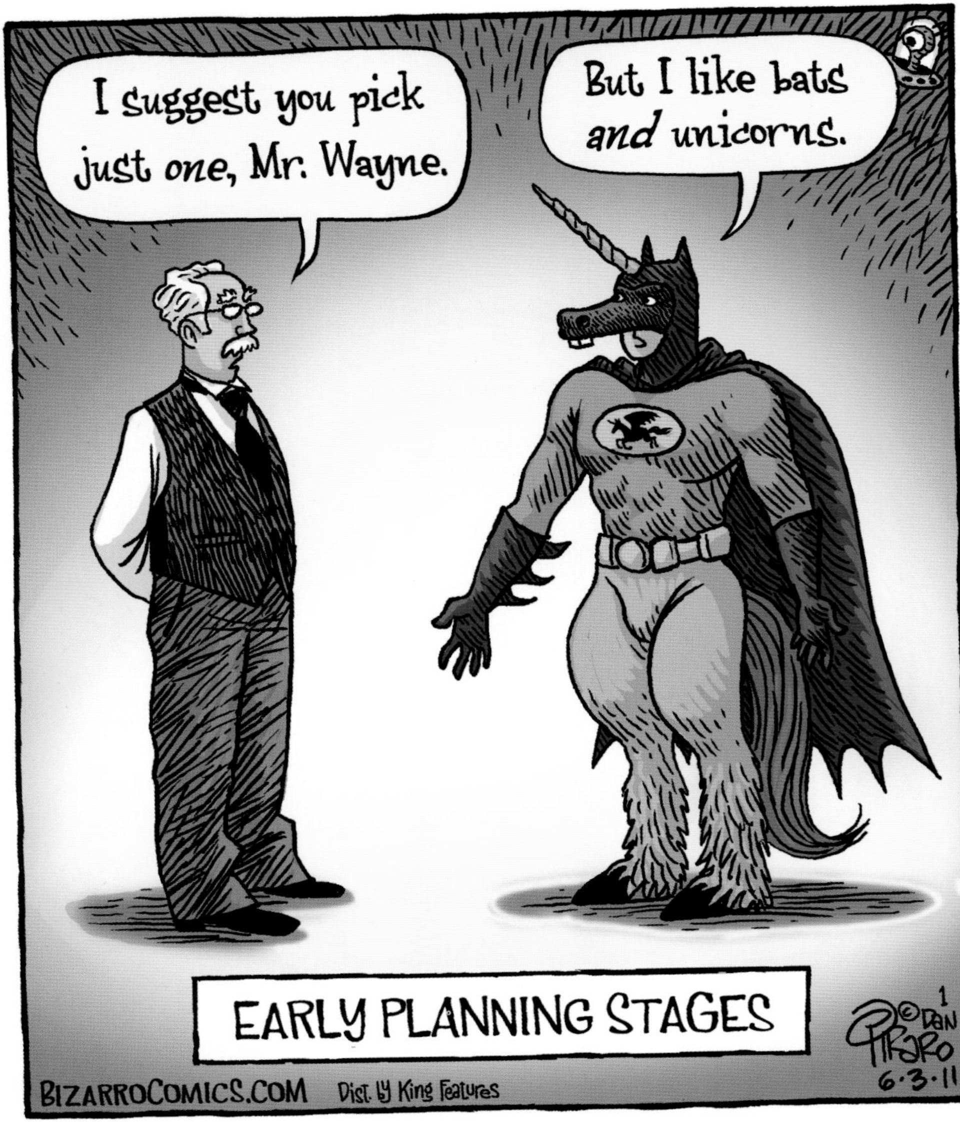
I suggest you pick just *one*, Mr. Wayne.
But I like bats *and* unicorns.
EARLY PLANNING STAGES
© DAN PIRARO 6·3·11
BIZARROCOMICS.COM
Dist. by King Features

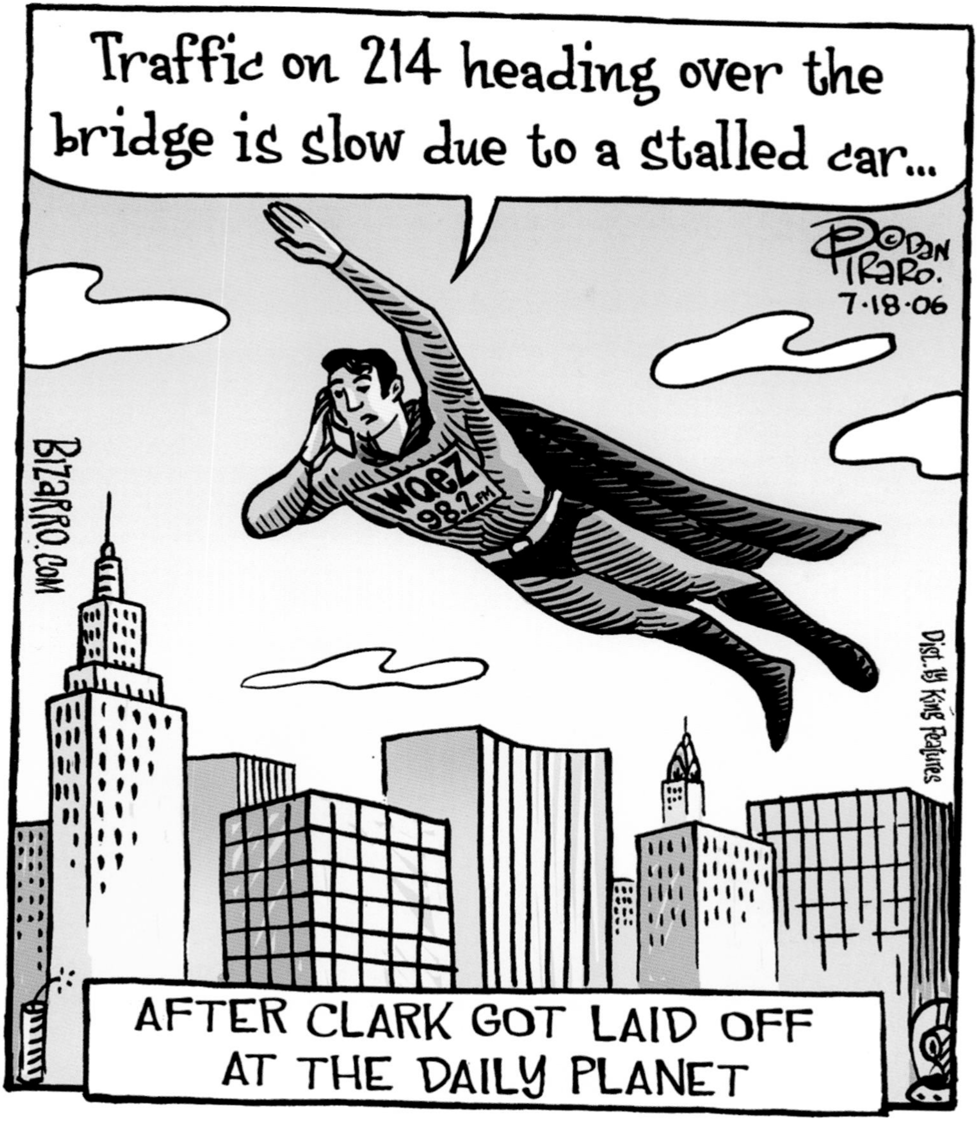
Traffic on 214 heading over the bridge is slow due to a stalled car...
WQEZ 98.2 FM
©DAN PIRARO. 7·18·06
BIZARRO.COM
Dist. by King Features
AFTER CLARK GOT LAID OFF AT THE DAILY PLANET

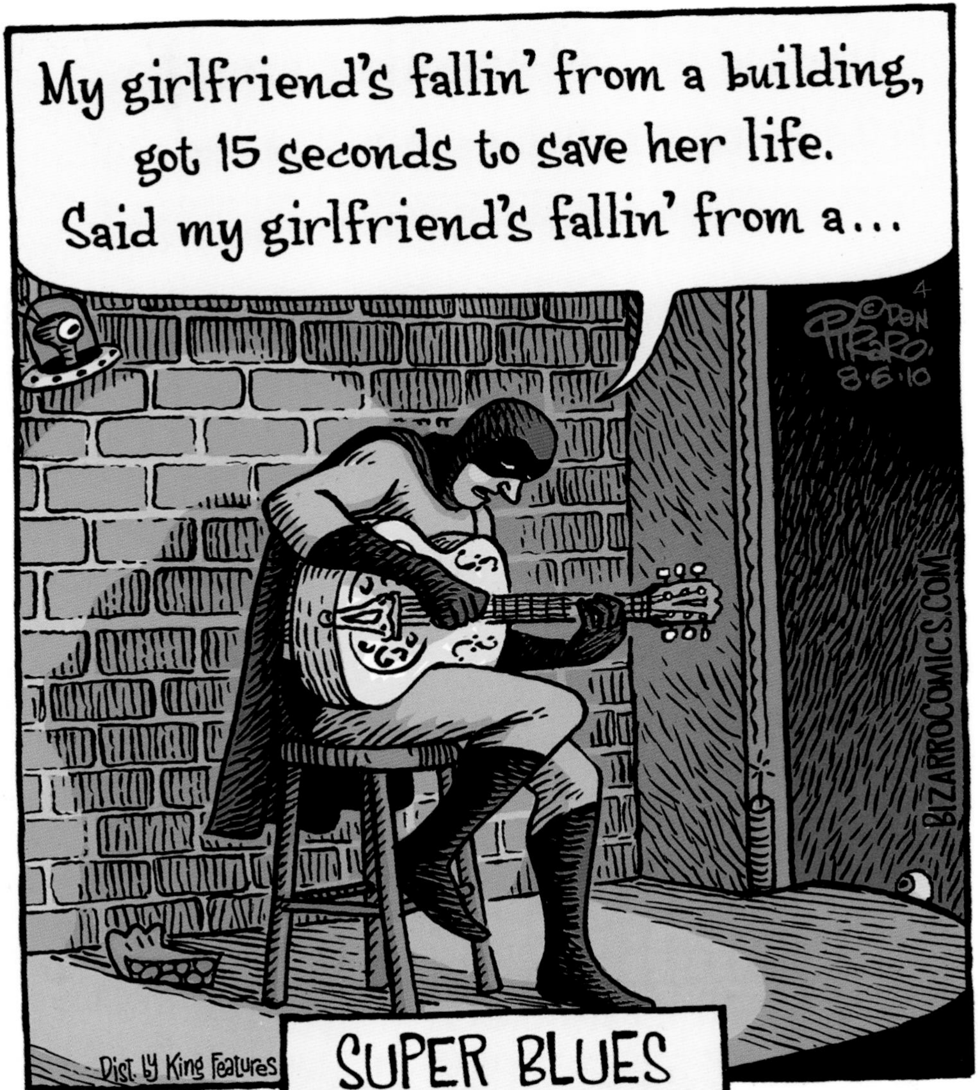
My girlfriend's fallin' from a building,
got 15 seconds to save her life.
Said my girlfriend's fallin' from a...
4
© DON PIRARO. 8·6·10
BIZARROCOMICS.COM
Dist. by King Features
SUPER BLUES

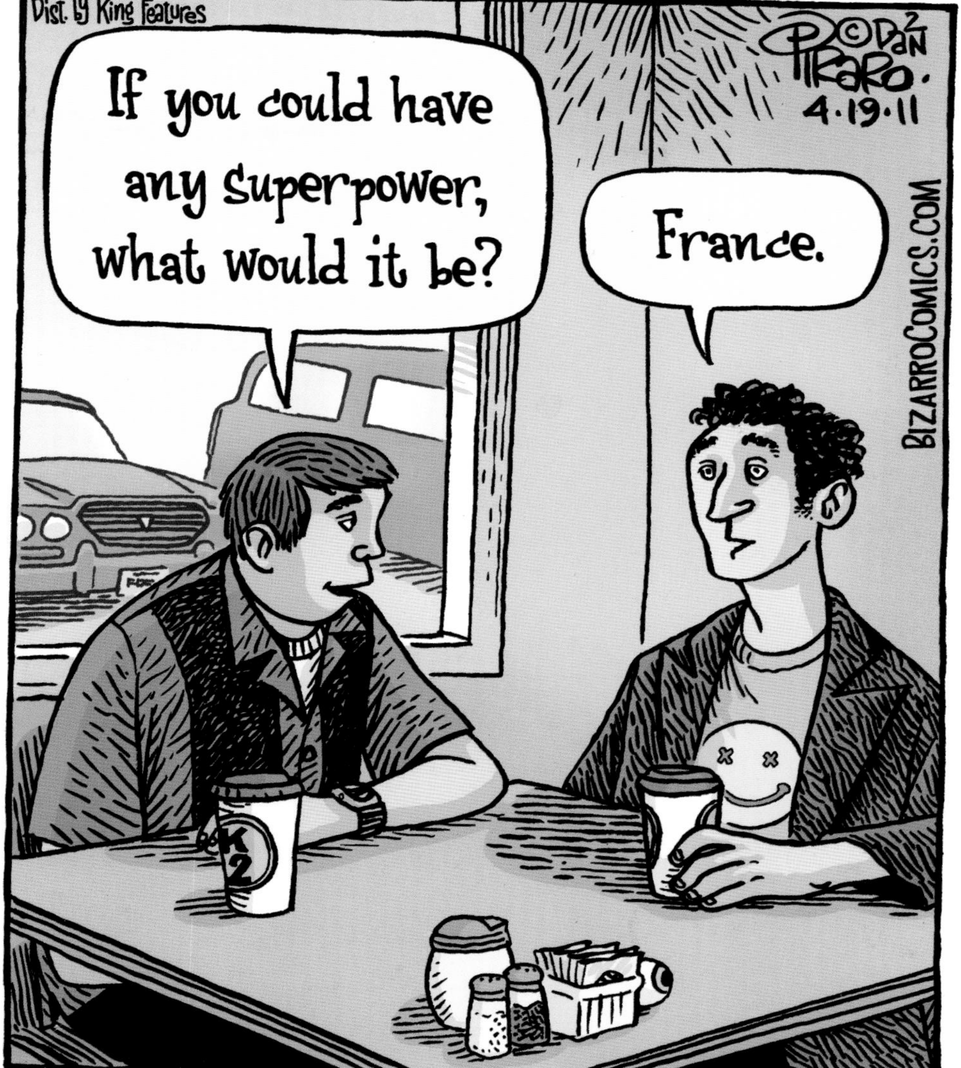
Dist. by King Features
©Dan Piraro. 4·19·11
If you could have any superpower, what would it be?
France.
BIZARROCOMICS.COM

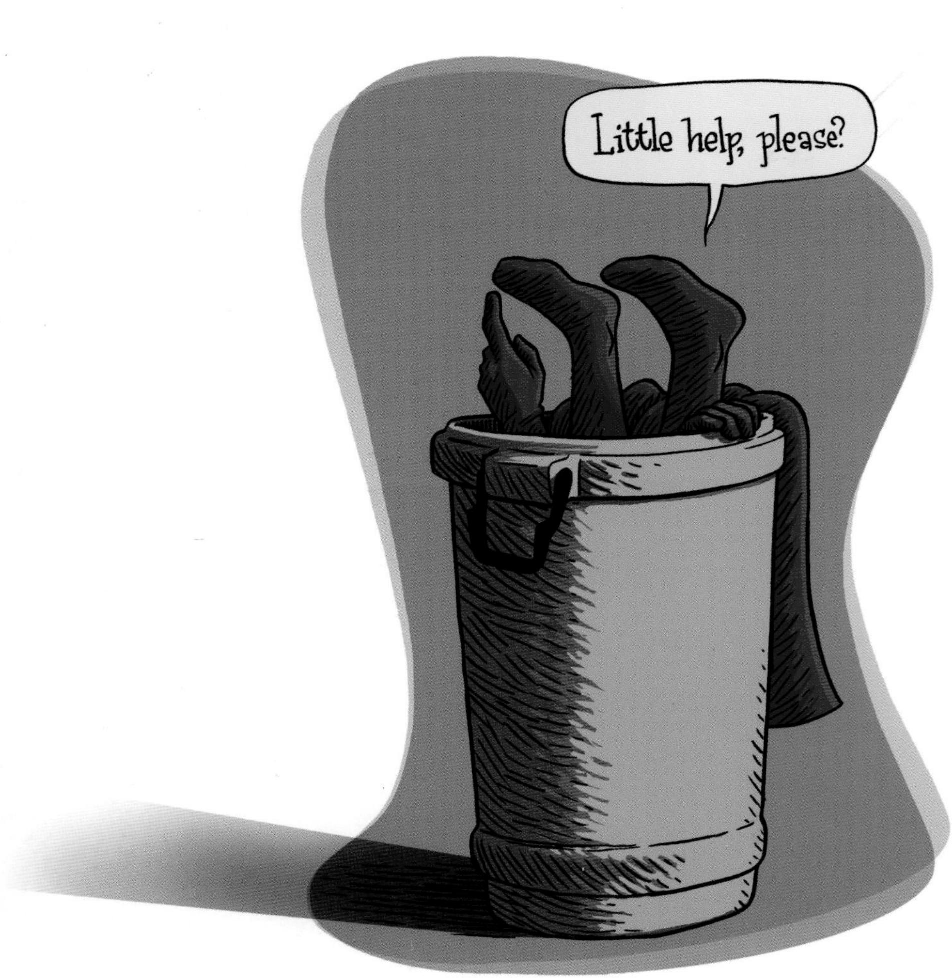
Little help, please?